REEL HISTORY

PATHWAYS PRESS

TABLE OF CONTENTS

INTRODUCTION

There's a moment in every movie where the lights sink, the room quiets, and something in the air shifts. It doesn't matter if you're in a packed cinema or curled up in front of a phone screen. There's this small breath before the story begins, that tiny pause where anything feels possible. That moment is older than Hollywood, older than color film, older than superheroes and streaming and binge nights. People felt it when they watched a grainy black-and-white train rush toward them in 1895. And they feel it now when a title card flashes across Netflix or a trailer drops on TikTok, and the whole internet stops for a second.

Movies have grown up with us. They've changed their shape, their sound, their swagger, their tools, their heroes. They've traveled the world, carried cultures on their backs, and reinvented themselves more times than a franchise that refuses to end. What's wild is how something that began as a flicker of light in a box turned into the most powerful storyteller humanity has ever had. And somehow, against all odds, it still feels new.

Think about how you watch movies today. A film from Japan can go viral in South Africa overnight. A Bollywood dance clip can spark a global challenge. A meme from an old French thriller can suddenly become everyone's favorite reaction GIF. A 90's blockbuster you've never heard of might show up because an algorithm thought you needed it. We live in a world where cinema isn't just a pastime. It's a language. A currency. A cultural heartbeat that moves faster than any studio exec could ever keep up with.

And that's part of the magic. Movies used to belong to Hollywood, but now they belong to everyone. Kids filming skits on their phones, creators breaking rules on YouTube, animators in their bedrooms sketching worlds that feel more alive than real life, and even fans who edit, remix, reimagine, and claim scenes like they're part of their own story. Film used to be locked behind expensive cameras and gated studios; today it's a very global playground that we're all invited into.

However, here's the twist: even though movies feel so modern, fast, and digital, they're built on a long trail of experiments, accidents, rebellions, and wild ideas. Every zoom, every meme-able frame, every dramatic entrance you love has roots somewhere, either unexpected, old, or somewhere bold. Cinema is basically a giant family tree where the branches keep growing into directions no one predicted.

Once you start noticing the connections, everything changes. Silent slapstick starts looking like TikTok humor. Early stop-motion suddenly feels like the blueprint for your favorite animated shows. Old-school monster movies start whispering inside modern blockbusters. Film movements from Italy, France, Japan, India, Nigeria, and South Korea echo in the movies you watch right now. They shaped the stories you love before you ever knew their names.

Perhaps that's why learning how movies evolved doesn't feel like digging through the past but more like unlocking a code to the present. It's like someone hands you a backstage pass and says, "Here, take a look at how the world learned to dream with pictures." Once you see how cinema got here, you'll never watch anything the same way again. Every shot becomes intentional. Every cut has meaning. Every trend has an ancestor. Every new film feels like it's carrying a spark from another era.

For a long time, film history was treated like some dusty academic thing. Thick textbooks filled with words no one uses in real life. Endless dates, endless names, barely any context, as if movies were invented by men in suits and then politely moved decade by decade until Marvel showed up. However, real film history is alive, messy, and full of chaos infused with risk, creativity, bad decisions, brilliant breakthroughs, and people who loved stories so much they refused to give up.

Look closely enough, and you'll see students experimenting with handheld cameras long before vlogs were a thing. You'll see directors arguing with studios, artists building worlds from cardboard, animators painting entire universes one frame at a time. You'll meet rebels who refused to follow the rules. Innovators who cracked open new genres. Outsiders who made space where there was none. Women, Black filmmakers, queer creators, global pioneers—people who weren't supposed to be in the story but pushed their way in anyway.

Cinema grew because people like them kept pushing, and it keeps growing because people like you keep watching, sharing, creating, questioning, and imagining. The story of movies is an ongoing conversation. Whether you're a teen just discovering classics, an anime lover obsessed with world-building, a streamer who binges everything in sight, or someone dreaming of directing, writing, editing, or animating someday, you're already part of that conversation.

Every generation redefines film in its own way. Yours is doing it louder, faster, and more globally than any before it. Movies no longer trickle from studios to the world. They pulse outward in waves of clips, edits, memes, reactions, reviews, duets, spoofs, remixes, tributes, and commentary. You don't just watch movies anymore; you participate in them and shape the culture around them.

So go ahead and settle in. Whether you're discovering film for the first time or deepening what you already love, there's room for you here. The past, the present, the streaming era, the fandom universe, the viral moments; they're all part of one long, continuous glow, and now you're stepping right into it. Welcome to the journey; Reel history starts now.

CHAPTER 1:

CHAPTER 1:

LIGHTS, CAMERA, ORIGINS!

"A day without laughter is a day wasted."
— Charlie Chaplin

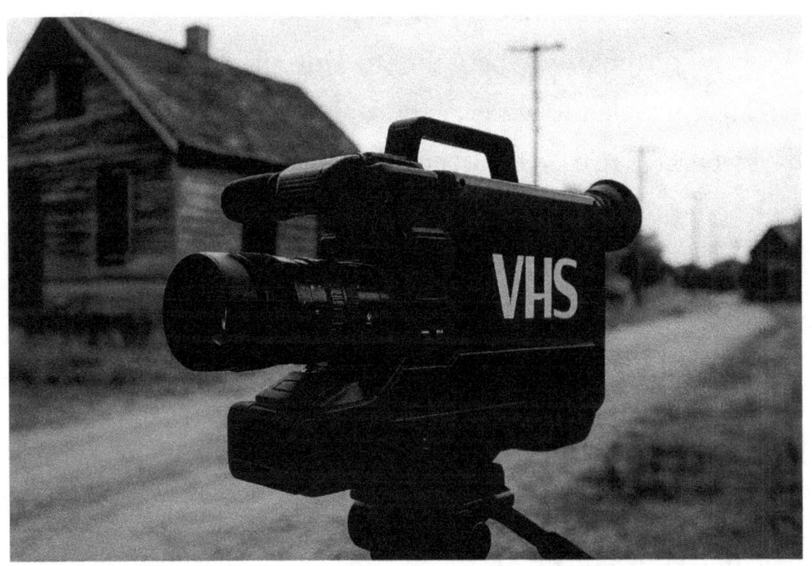

1895 → 1929

Imagine living in a world where nothing moves unless you're the one moving it. No videos. No GIFs. No looping edits or slow-motion replays. No anime fights, no music videos, no TikTok transitions, no K-drama cliffhangers, no "hold up, rewind that" moments. Just… stillness.

Now imagine someone in that world walking into a dark room and suddenly seeing a picture come alive. A horse running. A train charging toward them. Workers pouring out of a factory like they were real and right there. Not drawings or shadows, but actual, real people with real movement. It must have felt like witchcraft at the time, honestly, if not time travel or a glitch in reality.

That moment, that shock, that spark of "wait… how is this even possible" is where the story of cinema really begins.

Most people today never think about how wild those early days were. We're used to fast edits and 4K and CGI galaxies that look better than real life. However, the first people who watched moving pictures weren't casual viewers. They were witnesses. They were seeing the impossible crack open before them.

This chapter takes you right to that moment. Back to the first flickers of motion that changed everything. Back to the experiments, the accidents, the arguments, the discoveries, and the pure curiosity that made the world's greatest storytelling machine come alive.

Welcome to the real beginning of the movies before Hollywood, before sound, before color, and before all the rules. This is where cinema learned to take its first breath.

THE SPARK THAT STARTED EVERYTHING

Before we dive into the inventions and the breakthroughs, let's begin with a moment that feels familiar to anyone who has ever loved a movie. Think about the first time you saw a lightsaber glow across a dark screen, or the way a starship drifted through endless space in a Star Wars opening shot. Think about the weight of a Marvel battle scene, the kind where entire worlds bend under the force of imagination. These moments work because they make something impossible feel real.

Now, instead of jumping from moment to moment like a slideshow, let everything fade into one long timeline. Let all the big cinematic tricks, such as CGI blasts, motion-capture transformations, particle simulations, animated spells, and holographic interfaces, flow backward in one continuous sweep. Let it all blend into older tools: matte paintings, puppets, miniature models, hand-drawn frames, wires, layered glass, light tricks, shadows. Keep sliding back until you reach a world where none of it existed yet, a world where motion itself wasn't something anyone could capture. Not because people lacked imagination, but because the technology didn't exist.

That gap between imagination and possibility is where the spark began. Before cameras, film reels, projectors, and before electricity was consistent enough to rely on, there was simply a question floating in the air: Can movement be preserved? Not a drawing of movement or a description of movement, but actual movement. Could life be caught, held still, and then brought back whenever someone wanted to see it?

Modern filmmaking uses math, physics, coding, and design to create illusions that stretch reality. However, the earliest pioneers were dealing with an even more fundamental equation: how many still images does the brain need before those images stop feeling separate and start feeling alive? They didn't have software, but they had curiosity. They didn't have sensors and digital rigs, but they had persistence. And they weren't trying to build franchises or universes, but trying to solve a puzzle hidden inside human perception.

Look at any blockbuster today, like Star Wars, Marvel, anime epics, and high-budget fantasy, and you'll see layers of work that trace back to that first little spark. The spark wasn't special effects or editing tricks, Hollywood, fame, or billion-dollar studios. It was simply the urge to understand movement and share it with others.

Long before the first camera existed, the idea of recording motion was already haunting people's minds. They wanted to bottle time, to preserve moments, to let others witness something they otherwise would've missed. That desire is what gave birth to the path we're about to follow. Cinema began with curiosity, and that curiosity set everything else in motion.

THE FIRST FLICKERS

As we briefly established, the story of moving pictures doesn't begin with Hollywood or any fancy studio, it begins with a problem that haunted inventors, photographers, and scientists for decades. Everyone could take a picture, but no one could make that picture move. It sounds simple today, but in the late 1800s, it was like trying to invent teleportation. You had light, lenses, chemistry, and paper, but you couldn't make life replay itself.

Let's start with one of the funniest, most random scientific debates of the 1800s: Does a galloping horse ever lift all four hooves off the ground at the same time? Rich people argued about this like it was the Super Bowl. Some were convinced the horse always had one hoof on the ground. Others insisted there was a moment of full flight. Nobody could prove it because the motion was too fast for the human eye to detect.

Enter Eadweard Muybridge, a photographer with the patience of a monk and the vibe of someone who'd definitely invent a meme if he lived today. Muybridge set up *twelve* cameras along a racetrack, each rigged to fire when the horse ran past. When he placed the photos side by side, he created something no one had ever seen before: a sequence of captured motion. Not one picture or a painting, but an actual *series.*

And when those images were viewed quickly in order, the horse didn't just pose, it moved. The world froze for a second, and scientists got their answer (yes, all four hooves lift), then humanity got its first taste of animation. That tiny flipbook-style breakthrough would evolve into everything from anime to blockbuster action scenes.

While it wasn't cinema yet, it was the seed. Muybridge had basically invented the world's first GIF before computers existed.

Next in line was Thomas Edison, a man with two personalities: a brilliant inventor and an aggressive businessman. Edison wanted to go beyond animated photographs. He wanted a machine that would let a person watch moving pictures on demand. So he and his assistant, William Kennedy Dickson, created the Kinetoscope. Picture a wooden cabinet with a peephole at the top and a long strip of film running through it. You'd look inside and see tiny moving scenes: boxers sparring, dancers twirling, a man sneezing (yes, that was actually a hit at the time).

These films were short because the machine could only hold so much film. Basically, the Kinetoscope was a one-person cinema booth. Early content creators such as boxers, wrestlers, and vaudeville performers showed up to be filmed so their act could live inside these little devices. People lined up in arcades to watch these clips. It was addictive, exciting, and expensive. The only issue, though, was that you couldn't watch with friends. Edison wasn't interested in projection. He wanted to sell machines, not build community.

So while Edison was busy selling peephole devices, two brothers in France were working on something far more ambitious. Auguste and Louis Lumière created the Cinématographe, a camera that could record, develop, and project film. Three jobs in one. It was lighter, quieter, and frankly smarter than Edison's setup.

On December 28, 1895, they held the first public film screening in a Paris café basement. This wasn't a private booth or one viewer at a time, but a crowd gathered together, to watch the same moving image at the same moment.

Their first films were simple: workers leaving a factory, a baby eating, a train pulling into a station. Nothing fancy. But audiences weren't ready for even that. According to some reports, when the train on the screen moved toward the camera, people screamed, stumbled back, and even ducked. This wasn't because they were scared of trains, but because no one had ever seen a moving image projected with this kind of clarity. For the first time, a machine-made reality replayed itself.

Essentially, Muybridge demonstrated that motion could be captured. Edison proved it could be packaged and shown to individuals. The Lumière brothers revealed it could be shared with a crowd. Put those three together, and you've got the foundation of cinema: motion, mechanics, and community.

Now, every TikTok loop, every anime fight sequence, every Marvel battle, every YouTube vlog jump cut all trace back to these first flickers. The tools got bigger, prettier, and faster, but the core idea hasn't changed. You capture life, you replay it, you share it. That's the heart of movies,, which started with a photographer, an inventor, and two French brothers who didn't know they were building the future.

However, before projectors lit up big screens and before people lined up outside theaters, the world was already experimenting with light, illusion, and crowd-based storytelling. Cinema didn't drop out of the sky. It grew from a long trail of devices that tried to answer the same question in different ways: how do you make an image feel alive?

Where Magic Lanterns Actually Came From

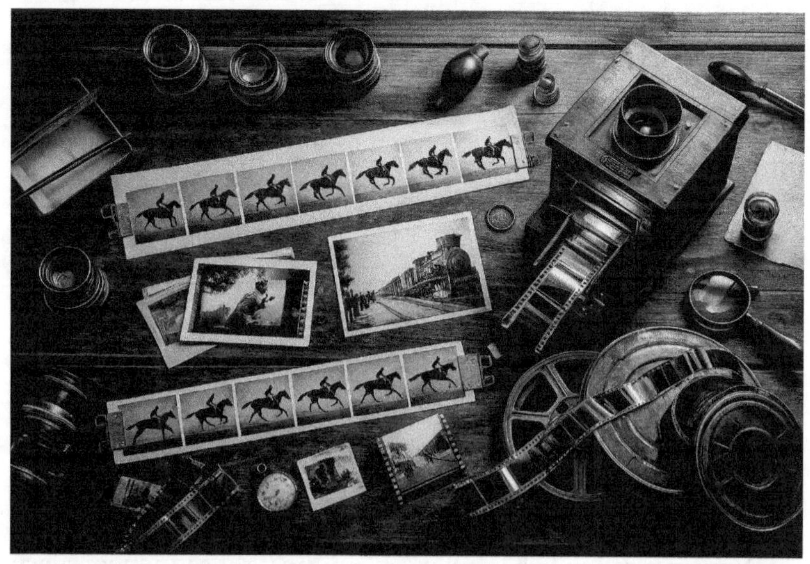

Magic lanterns didn't begin as entertainment machines. Their earliest roots stretch back to the 1600s, when scientists like Christiaan Huygens explored optics, lenses, and the behavior of light (*The Magic Lantern Society*, n.d.). People were fascinated by shadows and reflections, so experimenters built simple boxes that used bright lamps to project painted images onto walls. At first, it was mostly science, curiosity, and a bit of mischief. Only later did traveling performers, teachers, and storytellers turn these devices into full shows.

A magic lantern was a wooden box with a bright light inside and a glass slide at the front. The light passed through the slide, through a lens, and onto a wall or sheet. Nothing advanced. No cameras. No film strips. But when the room went dark, and an image glowed across the wall, people understood instantly that pictures could escape their frames. That idea alone prepared the world for cinema.

Lantern shows became gatherings where audiences laughed, gasped, argued, asked questions, shouted at presenters, and genuinely interacted with what they saw. Some slides had sliding pieces that made figures appear and disappear. Some presenters used two lanterns to transition between images. It was low-tech, but it taught audiences to expect spectacle.

Optical Toys - Early Lessons in Motion

Even with lanterns, people still craved movement. This craving led to an entire wave of optical toys in the 1800s. Thaumatropes, zoetropes, praxinoscopes, and flipbooks all relied on a simple discovery: if images change fast enough, the brain blends them into motion (*Victorian Optical Toys,* 2018). Kids spun cardboard disks and watched birds pop into cages. Families peered into spinning drums to see dancers twirl. These toys became the training ground for modern animation. They convinced the world that motion could be manufactured if you understood how the eye works.

In a way, these toys were the earliest form of loops. Today, we swipe through GIFs and quick edits. Back then, children spun drums and flipped pages. Essentially, it's different tools but the same instinct.

Penny Arcades

Once motion became something people expected, penny arcades capitalized on it. These noisy halls were filled with mechanical games, music boxes, and the first viewing machines that showed short films. Edison's Kinetoscope was the most famous. You dropped a coin into a cabinet, bent forward, and watched a tiny scene loop inside a peephole. The novelty worked, and people loved it, but then the experience remained isolated. One viewer per machine. No shared reactions, no group energy, no sense of community. It was fun, but it wasn't a cultural experience.

Nickelodeons

Everything changed when small storefront theaters started popping up around cities. These were nickelodeons. Five cents at the door. Films projected onto a screen. Wooden chairs arranged in rows. A pianist in the corner, doing their best to match the mood. For the first time, films were played for crowds. People walked in whenever they wanted, stayed as long as they felt like, and reacted together. Laughter spread, whispers jumped from row to row, and suspense felt heavier because everyone felt it at the same time. However, these rooms were loud, hot, and crowded, even if they made motion feel shared. That shift turned moving pictures from experiments into entertainment.

Nickelodeons exploded in popularity, and soon larger, more elaborate theaters appeared. Movie palaces: High ceilings, chandeliers, velvet curtains, ushers in uniform, orchestras warming up before the projection began. Walking into one felt like stepping into a dream.

People dressed up for the occasion. Families saved money for weekend shows. Moviegoing became a ritual, not just a pastime. Even the smell of popcorn became part of the experience. These spaces elevated film and turned simple moving pictures into cultural events.

However, as theaters grew, Edison attempted to control the entire filmmaking process through the use of patents. His company wanted every camera, projector, and film to run through him. Many independent filmmakers pushed back and moved west, looking for a place where they could work freely.

That journey leads to California and the birth of a certain famous industry, but that story belongs later in the book.

So the path from lanterns to theaters shows how storytelling moved from private tricks to public experiences. The technology improved, but the real transformation came from people gathering in dark rooms, reacting together, and turning films into a shared language.

Cinema wasn't just invented; it evolved, step by step, through curiosity, crowds, light, and a world that was learning how to dream out loud. Before long, those gatherings in dark rooms and the simple projected images began to raise a new question. If light and lenses could bring pictures to life, who would take the next step? Who would decide what stories were worth showing? Who would push the boundaries of what this new medium could do? Every invention attracts its pioneers, and once audiences learned to dream together, the door swung open for the people bold enough to shape those dreams.

Now that you've seen how early audiences learned to gather around moving light and how projection grew from a single viewer to a room full of people, it's time to meet the personalities who pushed this new medium forward. You've already caught glimpses of their names earlier in the chapter, almost like cameos, but this is where their full story unfolds.

THE OG CONTENT CREATORS: LUMIÈRE, MÉLIÈS, AND EDISON

The rise of early filmmakers can feel distant if you think of them only as historical figures. But the truth is that Lumière, Méliès, and Edison weren't so different from the teens posting edits, vlogs, skits, and short films today. They were working with tools that looked ancient compared to your phone, but the mindset was the same: tell a story, show people something new, put your own spin on reality, and hope it reaches an audience.

Lumière Brothers

Auguste and Louis Lumière ran a photography business before they ever touched moving pictures. When they created their device, the Cinématographe, they wanted to capture daily life as it was. Their short clips showed factory workers heading home, families sharing meals, and boats docking at harbors.

If you think about it, this is the same energy behind a "day in my life" vlog or a slice-of-life TikTok. No special effects, no acting, no script. Just life, recorded the way it happens.

What made the Lumière films powerful wasn't complexity but clarity. People saw themselves. They saw their neighbors. They saw movement that felt honest. The brothers chased authenticity, and somehow, that became spectacular.

Their screenings grew rapidly because people were curious about everyday moments, almost the same way viewers today scroll through relatable content. The Lumière brothers were basically the first documentary filmmakers, long before the term even existed.

Méliès

If the Lumières were the ancestors of vloggers and documentary creators, Georges Méliès was the grandfather of fantasy directors, editors, and VFX artists.

Méliès didn't want realism. He wanted imagination, magic, illusions, and impossible worlds. He started as a stage magician, which already tells you everything. When he accidentally discovered the substitution cut, where objects appear or disappear between frames, his mind went into overdrive. He painted sets, built props, designed costumes, and created effects that made audiences question their own eyes.

This is the man who sent a spaceship crashing into the moon's face in "A Trip to the Moon". He was doing green-screen energy before green screens existed. He hand-colored each frame of some films just to add vibrancy. Painstaking, but brilliant.

Today, you can create an effect on your phone with an app. Back then, Méliès created them from scratch, drawing on pure creativity and problem-solving. TikTok transitions, anime power-up sequences, Marvel explosions — all of them have some Méliès DNA in them. He wasn't just making films, he was building worlds.

That's when Thomas Edison came. He wasn't a filmmaker in the artistic sense, but he was the definition of a power player. His studio produced short films like "The Kiss" and "Fred Ott's Sneeze", and they were some of the first pieces of viral content. People paid to watch a sneeze. Imagine a world where someone's sneeze becomes premium content, and you have to drop a coin to view it. Edison made that happen. Edison resembles the modern studio executive or tech founder; someone who shapes the platform and the rules more than the content itself.

The coolest part is that these three pioneers represent instincts modern creators already have.

- Lumière energy: "Show people real life, capture moments, keep it relatable."
- Méliès energy: "Edit it, dramatize it, add effects, create something bigger than reality."
- Edison energy: "Build the system, set the rules, control the space where content lives."

Every teen creator today operates in one of these modes or blends of them. Some vlog, some animate, some edit, and others build entire fandoms or platforms. The tools have changed, but the creative drive hasn't.

Here's the wild part. Long before the internet, streaming, and social media, these creators still found a way to go viral.

Lumière films spread across Europe and beyond, projecting to packed crowds. Méliès' films traveled internationally and inspired remakes. Edison's films were copied, distributed, and even bootlegged. People weren't sharing links, they were sharing reels.

The world was smaller, which meant the tech was slower too, but the effect was the same: creators made things the world wanted to see, and the world found ways to spread them.

By the time filmmaking tools were in the hands of creators, audiences wanted more than moving pictures and clever tricks. They wanted personalities to follow and faces they recognized. Characters who made them laugh, gasp, or cheer without saying a single word. The world didn't know it yet, but it was about to meet cinema's first global celebrities: artists who turned body language into a superpower.

Charlie Chaplin

Chaplin didn't need dialog, flashy effects, or dramatic plot twists. He walked into a scene with a bowler hat, a bamboo cane, and those tiny, chaotic footsteps, and the entire audience lit up. His character, the Little Tramp, was funny, clumsy, hopeful, and brilliantly observant. In a world dealing with poverty, industrial change, and social struggle, he became a symbol of resilience.

Chaplin's comedy wasn't just slapstick. It was emotional timing. He could slip on a banana peel in one moment and deliver a gut punch of sincerity in the next. Teens today often say a TikTok "hits different" when humor and heart blend seamlessly; Chaplin mastered that long before phones, edits, or hashtags existed.

One of his most iconic bits, the bread roll dance, is basically a loopable meme in physical form. Two bread rolls, two forks, and a rhythm. Simple ingredients. Massive impact.

Buster Keaton

While Chaplin won hearts with emotion, Keaton stunned audiences with physics. Known as "The Great Stone Face," he kept a dead-serious expression even while chaos erupted around him. Keaton didn't just perform stunts. He engineered them.

This is the guy who stood still while a full-sized house facade collapsed around him and survived only because the window opening matched his exact height. No CGI or wires. Just precision, mathematics, and nerves of steel.

Keaton's films are still used in film schools because his timing and framing remain unmatched. Teens who love parkour videos, prank channels, or wild TikTok stunts would instantly connect with his style. He was doing extreme content creation long before anyone used that term.

Harold Lloyd

Lloyd brought a different flavor: optimism and athletic chaos. In "Safety Last!", he hangs from a clock tower high above a city street, fingers slipping as crowds scream below. That image alone is one of early cinema's most famous scenes.

What teens today don't always know is that Lloyd lost two fingers in an earlier stunt accident, yet kept performing. He risked more for a single laugh than most influencers would for an entire career. Lloyd was the cheerful chaos agent; confident, daring, and endlessly energetic.

So what all three shared was the power of visual storytelling. Their comedy didn't rely on language but on movement, timing, and the universal language of reaction. That's why it traveled across borders better than any modern franchise.

Think about:

- reaction memes
- GIFs
- POV humor
- TikTok skits without dialog
- animated comedy beats

All of these thrive because physical expression doesn't need translation.

Silent stars mastered that naturally.

Chaplin merchandise existed before Marvel merch. Keaton had global fan clubs. Movie magazines printed interviews, posters, and collectible cards. Kids copied their dances and gags the way teens today recreate TikTok trends. So these three men, with no sound, no color, and no digital effects, shaped the blueprint for how the world still reacts to visual comedy today.

Once movies learned to move people, they didn't stay in one country. Silent cinema didn't spread slowly the way inventions usually do. It jumped borders, languages, and cultures almost instantly. And because no one needed subtitles or translation, audiences everywhere could follow the stories, feel the jokes, and cheer for the heroes. This was the first time in history that one art form united the world in real time.

Japan

Before Japan even had a large-scale film industry, it had something Hollywood didn't: the **benshi**. A benshi was a live narrator who stood beside the screen and performed the movie as it played. They explained the plot, voiced every character, and added comedy, drama, suspense, and emotion. Some benshi became celebrities in their own right (Jivkova, 2021).

This meant Japanese audiences weren't just watching films. They were watching a hybrid performance, a mix of cinema and theater. So since benshi shaped the mood, Japanese films began to develop a style that felt more expressive and dramatic.

Action scenes, samurai stories, and early ninja films played well in this system. The visuals carried the movement, and the benshi carried the emotion. In a way, it mirrors how streamers today talk over gameplay or how reaction YouTubers guide the energy of what you're watching.

Russia

Meanwhile, Russia approached cinema with the mindset of engineers and philosophers. Filmmakers like Sergei Eisenstein believed that editing wasn't just a tool. It was the heart of cinema. They argued that two ordinary shots, when placed together, could create a meaning greater than either shot alone.

This led to the invention of **montage**, a technique that shapes nearly every movie and TikTok edit today.

In films like *Battleship Potemkin*, Eisenstein cut between crowds, soldiers, close-ups, and wide shots to build tension and emotion. The famous "Odessa Steps" sequence remains one of the most studied scenes in film history for its powerful use of rhythm, timing, and contrast.

Modern creators who make hype edits, emotional vlogs, anime-style transitions, or dramatic sports montages are working with principles Eisenstein defined nearly a century ago.

India

In India, cinema found its spark through Dadasaheb Phalke. After seeing a silent film from abroad, he became obsessed with creating films based on Indian stories. The result was *Raja Harishchandra* in 1913, a film rooted in mythology, family, honor, and faith.

Indian audiences connected with it instantly. Not because of the technology, but because the story felt personal and culturally familiar. This is the foundation of what would eventually grow into Bollywood and the world-famous Indian film industry.

The early films were full of elaborate costumes, expressive acting, and storytelling on a larger-than-life scale; elements that evolved into the spectacle-driven style India is known for today.

Silent cinema also grew in:

- **Egypt**, where early studios formed the roots of Arab cinema.

- **Nigeria**, where traveling theater and early photographers set the stage for Nollywood decades before the industry had a name.
- **China**, where filmmakers like Ruan Lingyu helped create a wave of melodramatic and socially aware films.
- **France**, beyond Méliès, with studios experimenting in fantasy, science fiction, and early fashion films.

Most countries were building their own visions of what moving pictures could be rather than just waiting for Hollywood.

The key advantage was silence. Without language barriers, films moved as freely as light. A funny gag in New York made people laugh in Tokyo. A dramatic chase in Russia thrilled an audience in Egypt. A mythological story from India felt universal even to people who had never heard the language.

Cinema became the world's first shared visual language. So when you scroll through your feed, you'll see:

- anime edits
- K-drama clips
- Bollywood scenes
- Nollywood memes
- Russian workout montages
- Japanese reaction content

Young people today consume global cinema daily without even noticing. That instinct to enjoy stories across borders started in the silent era. Before sound arrived, movies had already become global. People were learning to dream together, even from opposite ends of the planet.

SILENT ERA

However, filmmakers still had to convince audiences that magic could exist on screen. They had no shortcuts, no presets, no toolkits waiting in a menu. What they did have was imagination strong enough to challenge what a camera could capture, and somehow, with nothing but paint, glass, scissors, tape, clever angles, and patience, they pulled it off. The silent era didn't rely on technology; it relied on creativity, fearless enough to challenge physics.

We met Georges Méliès earlier, but this is where his work truly comes into focus. Méliès used cinema the way an artist uses a sketchbook. He cut film strips, glued frames, painted backgrounds, and layered images by hand. Every illusion was a puzzle, and he figured out the solutions one experiment at a time.

One of his most famous discoveries happened by accident. His camera jammed during a street shoot. When he fixed it and continued filming, the objects in front of the camera had changed. When he developed the footage, it looked like things appeared and vanished instantly. Instead of panicking, he saw an opportunity.

This became the **substitution splice**, one of the first special effects in film history. Today, you can recreate that same effect with a simple pause button. Back then, it felt like wizardry.

Double Exposure

Filmmakers learned that if they rewound the film and recorded over it again, they could place multiple images in the same frame. This created ghosts, clones, glowing spirits, and supernatural illusions.

Modern creators use double exposure for dreamy transitions, personality edits, surreal overlays, and music-driven aesthetic videos. Silent-era directors used it to make people float, disappear, multiply, or turn transparent.

Stop-Motion

Later on, Filmmakers experimented with stop-motion. They moved objects a little at a time, taking a picture between each movement. When played quickly, the illusion of motion appeared. Toys danced, chairs slid across floors, and dolls came to life.

If you've ever watched a LEGO stop-motion video or animated a character frame by frame in an app, you're using the same principles silent-era filmmakers discovered while figuring things out on the fly.

Miniatures — Tiny Worlds With Big Impact

Building full-sized sets was expensive, so many filmmakers used miniatures. Small buildings, toy trains, cardboard cities, and hand-crafted landscapes helped create scenes too large to build in real life.

Model-making is still used today in films like *Star Wars*, *Inception,* and *The Dark Knight.* But the silent era used miniatures with even fewer resources, relying on perspective and lighting to sell the illusion.

Matte Paintings

Artists painted entire landscapes or architecture on glass sheets and positioned them in front of the camera. The real actors filled part of the frame. The painting filled the rest. This created the illusion of castles, cities, or mountains far beyond the limits of the set. It's the ancestor of digital backgrounds used in animation, CGI films, and virtual production today.

Silent-era filmmakers learned that placing objects closer or further from the camera changed their apparent size. With this trick, a small prop could look enormous or a large object could appear tiny.

If you've ever taken a photo where someone "holds up" a building or "crushes" a friend's head between their fingers, you've used the same trick.

Modern VFX can create anything, but silent-era effects teach a lesson every creator needs: tech doesn't make the magic. Creativity does. These filmmakers built illusions by studying how the eye works and how the brain fills in gaps. They were designers, problem-solvers, and engineers without formal titles. For instance, if you want to recreate a classic Méliès vanish effect:

1. Record someone standing in place.
2. Pause the recording.
3. Have them step out of the frame.
4. Resume recording.

When you play it back, they will appear and vanish instantly.

That's the same idea Méliès used, but now it takes seconds instead of scissors and glue.

So the silent-era effects remind us that filmmaking didn't begin with machines doing the work. It began with people willing to invent solutions, manipulate light, and take risks to bring imagination to life. It wasn't about the tools. It was about seeing what could happen if you bent the rules of reality just enough to make the audience believe.

THE WORLD BEFORE SOUND

So by the time the silent era reached its peak, filmmakers had already proven something remarkable. Without recorded voices, soundtracks, dialog, and microphones hidden in props, they built an entire language out of light and movement. Every expression, camera, every angle cut, and every stunt was part of a growing vocabulary that the world was learning together.

What makes this period so special isn't just that it came first, it's that nothing about it was easy. Everything we take for granted now had to be invented by someone who didn't yet know the rules. Or better yet, someone who decided rules didn't matter.

When we scroll through TikTok today, react to anime edits, laugh at visual memes, or binge a movie without thinking twice about subtitles or sound design, we're using instincts filmmakers developed in silence. Those instincts came from people who relied on creativity instead of technology, intention instead of noise.

What the silent era teaches us is simple: movies were never about the tools. They were about the imagination behind them. Limitations didn't shrink cinema, they pushed it forward.

Silent films laid the foundation that every modern story stands on. They taught us how to feel through images, how to follow motion, how to read emotion without words. They taught directors how to guide attention, actors how to communicate with the eyes and editors how to shape time.

And then, just when filmmakers had mastered the art of silence, something unexpected was about to hit the world. A new invention. A new risk. A new chapter that would change everything again.

The movies were about to find their voice.

CHAPTER 2:

THE WORLD OF SOUND

"You ain't heard nothin' yet!"
— The Jazz Singer (1927)

1927 → 1939

Imagine watching a movie where the world holds its breath. No footsteps, no whispered warnings, no heartbeat in the soundtrack to tell you that danger is coming. No rustling leaves, no door creak, no sudden sting of music before something jumps out. Just images… and your mind filling in the rest.

If you've ever watched *A Quiet Place*, you already know how powerful that kind of silence can be. In that film, every tiny sound matters. Every breath feels risky. Every movement feels louder than it should. Silence becomes its own form of tension, its own kind of language.

Now imagine that being the normal state of cinema for an entire era. That's the world movies were born into.

Silent films weren't silent because filmmakers wanted silence. They were silent because there was no reliable way to record a voice, sync it to moving images, amplify it for a crowd, or play it back without something breaking. But that didn't mean the world of early cinema was quiet.

People today picture silent film screenings like museums: quiet, serious, almost sacred. The reality was the total opposite. A silent film screening could be louder than a modern action movie.

There was always a pianist, sometimes a violinist, sometimes an entire orchestra if the theater had the money. People clapped, gasped, whispered, argued, cheered, and occasionally threw popcorn when they disagreed with what happened on screen. Projectionists added sound effects by hand. Some theaters had employees behind the screen banging pots to mimic thunder or shaking metal sheets to create storms. In other terms, silence was a canvas.

The early filmmakers had mastered motion. They had mastered pacing, emotion, comedy, and even special effects. But every time they watched their own films, something felt missing. Life didn't move quietly, and people talked, cities buzzed, footsteps echoed, doors slammed, animals roared, and crowds cheered.

Adding sound, though, was a nightmare. Not a single part of the filmmaking process was built for it. Microphones picked up everything, even the camera motors that whirred loudly during filming. Actors couldn't move freely because stepping out of the microphone's range meant losing the audio. Lights hummed too loudly, sets echoed, recording devices broke easily, and even if you recorded something usable, playing it back in sync with the film was almost impossible.

Imagine trying to sync audio to a TikTok video without any editing tools. Now imagine trying to sync it for a whole movie, for a crowd of hundreds, using equipment that overheated, snapped, or jammed. That's the challenge filmmakers were facing.

So before the world officially heard a movie, there were dozens of attempts to fuse sound and image.

Inventors tried:

- musicians syncing live performances with film reels
- early sound-on-disc machines spinning beside the projector
- phonographs hidden under the screen
- crude microphones that amplified more noise than dialog

None of it was reliable. Every attempt failed in some dramatic fashion. Sometimes the audio lagged or sped ahead, and sometimes the machine jammed completely. However, every failure pushed filmmakers a little closer.

Here's a twist most teens don't expect: not everyone was excited about sound, though. Some directors believed sound would ruin the purity of visual storytelling. Some actors feared audiences would hate their real voices. Theater owners worried they would have to buy expensive new equipment, and musicians feared losing their jobs.

So this sparked a real debate: should movies stay silent?

However, art rarely stands still. The question wasn't whether sound would arrive but who would be brave enough to make it work. Then, when it finally worked, the entire industry changed forever.

THE JAZZ SINGER

The moment sound finally worked on film, it didn't feel like the industry was slowly unlocking a new feature. It felt like someone broke open the sky. After years of false starts, failed experiments, and equipment that refused to behave, the breakthrough arrived in a single night that didn't look dramatic on the outside but shook the entire world underneath it.

Critics had seen sound experiments before. Audiences had heard music syncing attempts before. Inventors had made bold promises that never delivered. But none of those moments had the spark or the clarity needed to convince people that synchronized sound could truly live inside a movie.

Then came '*The Jazz Singer.*'

When people walked into the Warner Bros theater in October 1927, they expected another clever experiment. They expected a few sound effects, maybe a speech that drifted in and out of sync. They clearly didn't expect a moment that would make history feel like it was rewinding and rewriting itself (Pfeiffer, n.d.).

The film begins like many others of the time, with silent scenes accompanied by music. But halfway through, the lead actor, Al Jolson, looks up from the piano and speaks directly to his mother. His voice is smooth, clear, and undeniably human.

"You ain't heard nothing yet."

People in the audience froze. Some leaned forward, unsure if they were imagining it. Others started whispering. For the first time, a character on screen spoke in a way that matched his movement, expression, and emotion.

The world had grown used to the language of silence. Audiences had learned how to read faces, follow expressions, and feel emotions through movement alone, but hearing a real voice inside the story created a shock that modern audiences can only compare to the first time VR felt real or the first time the internet connected people in real time. It pushed cinema beyond illusion.

Suddenly, a fictional world felt less like a projection and more like something breathing on the other side of the screen, the emotional weight rising with the sound of a human voice and the performances shifting into a new kind of depth as scenes carried a fuller presence that audiences had never experienced before. In that moment, everyone understood the industry had crossed a line it would never step back from.

Think of what it feels like the first time a creator you follow reveals their voice after posting silent content for months. Or when a livestream shows them laughing in real time, instead of typing. That transition creates a deeper connection. It feels more sincere, more vivid, and more personal.

That's exactly what audiences felt that night in 1927.

Instead of a few thousand followers watching a screen on their phones, it was millions of people across the world watching cinemas evolve before their eyes.

Studios reacted almost instantly and the mood swung in every direction as some celebrated the breakthrough, others panicked about what it meant for their future, a few tried to downplay the impact and insist that silence still had a place, yet the shift had already happened because once audiences heard a voice that matched the movement on screen, everything filmmakers believed about storytelling was suddenly in motion, reshaping itself in real time.

Actors would have to adjust. Directors would have to change their methods. Sets would need to be rebuilt. Technology would have to evolve. Budgets would rise. Entire careers would disappear or be born overnight.

The rules had changed. Forever.

HOLLYWOOD IN CHAOS

When *The Jazz Singer* shattered the silence, Hollywood didn't slip into this new era gracefully. It stumbled into it. The moment sound proved it could work, every studio looked at their equipment, their actors, their stages, and their wallets and realized they were completely unprepared. Silent films were built on freedom: moving cameras, expressive acting, improvisation, outdoor shoots, and directors barking instructions mid-scene. Sound didn't just add a new feature; it rewired the entire system.

Microphones

Early microphones were ridiculously sensitive. They picked up camera noise, footsteps, the rustle of clothing, background chatter, and even the hum of studio lights. The only thing they struggled with was capturing clean dialog.

Actors suddenly had to stand very still, with their heads tilted toward hidden microphones inside plants, telephones, or lamps. If an actor moved too far, the sound faded. If they moved too quickly, they drifted out of range. I'm sure this was exciting for actors at the time because directors who were used to shouting directions during a take now had to stay silent because their voice could be picked up, too.

The result was stiff performances and scenes that felt chained to the microphone's position. Hollywood went from expressive physical acting to something that looked more like filmed theater.

Cameras

Silent-era cameras made an incredible amount of noise. No one cared before because the films didn't record sound, but the moment sound became necessary, the cameras became a problem.

To solve this, studios stuffed cameras into giant wooden boxes called "blimps." These blimps muffled the noise but turned cameramen into trapped operators sweating inside a cramped coffin-shaped structure. Moving the camera became nearly impossible.

Filmmakers who built their style on motion now had to accept still, locked-off shots. It was a creative limitation that made many directors feel like they had gone backward rather than forward.

Sets Rebuilt Overnight

Silent studios weren't designed with sound in mind, which meant floors creaked, walls echoed, and ceilings let whatever noise drifted in from outside leak in, all problems no one cared about when films relied entirely on visuals. Directors and actors talked freely during takes because nothing was recording their voices, a habit that suddenly became impossible the moment sound arrived and every stray noise threatened to slip into the scene.

Studios tore apart their stages and rebuilt them with soundproof walls. They created sealed rooms for recording dialog. They rewired electrical systems, built quiet lights, purchased new cameras, and learned entirely new workflows.

This wasn't a small upgrade. It was the industry equivalent of switching from bicycles to airplanes in a single year.

Actors

Some silent stars depended on expressive faces and grand gestures. Their charisma came from movement, not speech, so when audiences finally heard their voices, the reaction wasn't always what studios hoped for. John Gilbert, one of the era's biggest romantic leads, struggled because his voice didn't match the suave screen persona audiences were used to. Clara Bow, the original "It Girl," ran into a different challenge — her strong Brooklyn accent clashed with the glamorous image studios built around her. Even Buster Keaton faced setbacks, not because of his voice, but because sound limited the physical style that made his work so special.

On the other hand, some actors flourished. Greta Garbo's accent became part of her mystique, turning her first spoken line, "Garbo talks," into a major cultural moment. Maurice Chevalier charmed audiences instantly with his voice, leaning into musical roles that made him even more popular.

This was the first time in Hollywood's history that technological change erased careers overnight while launching others into new levels of fame.

Directors

Directors who had mastered silent storytelling now had to learn timing based on spoken lines rather than gestures. Scenes couldn't be edited with the same rhythm because dialog needed room to breathe. Shots had to match sound cues, and performances had to sync.

Furthermore, since early sound made cameras difficult to move, directors lost one of their favorite tools: motion. It was creativity under constraint, a challenge filmmakers today understand when they try to shoot something with limited gear.

Sound-On-Disc vs Sound-On-Film

At first, no one agreed on the best way to record audio. Some studios used sound-on-disc systems where a record played alongside the projector, hoping the two machines stayed perfectly in sync. If the film slipped even slightly, the voice drifted out of sync, and the illusion shattered.

Others pushed for sound-on-film technology, in which sound waves were recorded directly onto the film strip using light. This method was more stable and eventually became the standard, but in the early years both systems were competing aggressively. Projectionists had to learn new techniques. Theaters had to install speakers and amplifiers. Engineers had to invent new ways to boost volume without distorting the sound. It was a revolution that demanded new skills from every corner of the industry.

So even though everything felt uncertain, one thing was clear: sound was the new foundation. Filmmakers who adapted gained power, and audiences who heard a character whisper, laugh, or sing on screen didn't want to go back.

Essentially, silent cinema had taught film how to move, but sound taught it how to breathe. New possibilities arrived, new atmospheres formed, and entire categories of cinema became possible for the first time. This is when something called a *genre* was established. The word *genre* comes from the French term for "type" or "kind," but in film it means something deeper (*What Is Genre?*, n.d.) A genre shapes how a movie feels, how it behaves, and what the audience expects the moment the opening scene fades in.

Silent films had genres too, but the lack of spoken dialog and recorded sound limited them. Once sound entered the picture, it didn't simply enhance old genres, it unlocked new ones.

GENRES

Imagine trying to make a musical without music. A detective thriller without whispered confessions. A rapid-fire comedy without overlapping dialog. These ideas simply wouldn't function the same way in silence. Sound didn't replace visual storytelling; it expanded its vocabulary. Filmmakers now had voices to play with, rhythm to shape scenes, music to set the mood, and sound cues to direct emotion. This opened the door to creative territories that had been impossible a few years earlier.

Musicals

The arrival of sound turned musicals into a natural fit for film. Audiences didn't just watch performances anymore but felt them. Songs carried emotion, dance numbers came alive, and the screen suddenly became a stage that reached millions.

Early musicals weren't always smooth. Some were basically filmed in a theater, with stiff staging and limited camera movement. However, as filmmakers adapted, musicals became some of the most imaginative works of the era. They blended story, performance and rhythm in ways no silent film could.

Gangster Films

As filmmakers experimented with what sound could do, certain stories seemed almost designed for this new dimension. Crime films were one of the first to transform. In silence, crime stories relied on shadows, chases, and visual tension, but the moment sound arrived, a different kind of energy crept in. The click of a gun being cocked, the echo of footsteps in an alley, the smug confidence in a criminal's voice — these elements shifted crime from suspenseful visuals to something sharper and more atmospheric.

Films like *Little Caesar* (1931) and *The Public Enemy* (1931) were early examples that showed how dialog could carve out personality. Actors like Edward G. Robinson and James Cagney didn't just play gangsters, they sounded like them. Their accents, rhythm, and delivery created characters who felt dangerous even before they pulled a weapon.

Sound shaped how audiences perceived these worlds. The roughness of a voice could reveal authority, the tone of a threat could define a villain, and the rhythm of an argument could carry more tension than a chase. Early gangster films created iconic archetypes: the smooth-talking villain, the tough street boss, the fast-paced shootout echoing through dark alleys. Sound didn't just enhance these stories; it defined them.

Screwball Comedies

Screwball comedies exploded because sound made rapid-fire dialog possible. These films relied on quick banter, misunderstandings, overlapping lines, and verbal chaos. The humor wasn't just physical anymore — it came from timing, rhythm, and the unexpected ways characters bounced off each other.

This style still thrives today in films, sitcoms, and even fast-talking YouTube or TikTok creators who use timing as their punchline.

Essentially, genres guide expectations in the same way playlists guide mood. You know what you're getting into the moment you choose one. And once sound became part of the cinematic language, these genres formed identities strong enough to last for decades.

WHEN SOUND WENT GLOBAL AND CINEMA LEARNED TO ADAPT

When sound settled into Hollywood, the excitement and chaos didn't stay within American borders. The moment voices, music, and real-world sound effects hit the screen, the world reacted — sometimes with awe, sometimes with confusion, and sometimes with a long list of technical problems that made filmmakers wonder if silence had been easier. But one thing was certain: sound turned film into a global conversation, and every country answered in its own way.

The Global Ripple

Every region adapted sound differently because every culture valued sound differently. Some countries leaned into music, whereas others leaned into theatrical traditions. Some resisted the change at first, while others embraced it immediately (Cook and Sklar, 2025).

In Germany, filmmakers experimented with sound to build atmosphere and psychological tension. Their early sound films drifted toward dark lighting, expressive shadows, and moods that would later influence film noir. Meanwhile, France embraced sound through poetry and romance. Dialog became a way to explore relationships and emotion rather than speed and spectacle.

In Japan, sound had to compete with a beloved tradition that already existed around film: the *benshi*. When sound films arrived, benshi culture resisted at first because recorded dialog replaced their role. Japan took longer to transition because removing the benshi meant reshaping the identity of their film experience.

India, on the other hand, launched itself forward immediately because sound allowed filmmakers to blend stories, music, and performance; a natural extension of Indian storytelling traditions. The early sound era helped shape what would become Bollywood's vibrant style.

The result was a world in motion, each region redefining what sound could mean.

Multilingual Film

The moment film introduced spoken dialog, Hollywood faced a new issue: not everyone spoke English. Subtitles were not yet efficient, and dubbing technology was inconsistent at best, so studios tried something that now sounds absolutely wild: they made multiple versions of the same movie in different languages.

The same set, the same costumes, the same lighting, but different actors performing the same script in Spanish, French, German, or whatever region the studio wanted to reach. Some crews worked overnight, filming their version once the English-speaking cast went home.

It was exhausting, expensive, and short-lived, but it proved something important: film had become global, and studios knew it.

So the arrival of sound changed how people behaved in theaters. Audiences couldn't talk through films anymore because dialog mattered. Theaters dimmed lights strategically to keep attention on the screen. People leaned in during whispered scenes. Songs stuck in people's heads after they left. The relationship between the audience and the film became more intimate. This shift was especially clear in films that poked fun at early sound itself.

Singin' in the Rain

If there is one film teens should watch to understand the chaos of Hollywood's transition to sound, it's *Singin' in the Rain*. Even though it was made decades later, it captures the confusion, panic, and accidental comedy that studios faced during those early years.

It shows microphones hidden inside clothing. Actors frozen in place because they couldn't step away from a mic. Dialog echoing awkwardly because no one knew how to record it cleanly. Entire scenes ruined by a single loud noise in the background, and of course, those disastrous early test screenings proved how unprepared the industry was. *Singin' in the Rain* is more than entertainment; it's a historical mirror held up to the talkie revolution.

By the time sound settled into the global film industry, cinema had changed forever. It became a blend of voice, music, rhythm, noise, and performance. Countries found their own ways to adapt, audiences discovered new ways to feel stories, and filmmakers realized they were standing at the edge of a much larger creative landscape. The world had learned to hear the movies, and it would never un-hear them again.

WATCH, TRY, EXPLORE

The transition from silence to sound didn't unfold like a neat chapter in a history book. It arrived as a wave that was loud, messy, confusing, and unstoppable, reshaping every corner of filmmaking. The silent era had taught directors how to move the camera, build emotion through expression, and guide attention through editing. But when sound arrived, the rules shifted. Dialog added personality. Music added depth. Voices added vulnerability. The screen didn't just show life anymore; it started sounding like it.

What makes this moment so powerful is that filmmakers didn't step forward with perfect technology or complete confidence. They stepped forward with risk. Some careers blossomed, others faded, but the art form itself grew. Sound simply expanded the silent era, and once audiences heard characters speak, sing, or whisper, cinema opened into a new dimension that still shapes every story told today.

As we move forward into a time when color reshapes the image, and Hollywood its Golden Age, the echoes of this transition stay with us. Sound taught cinema to speak, and now it was ready to dream in full color.

Explore the sound revolution through clips, activities, and reflections you can jump into at your own pace.

1. Watch This Next

- *The Jazz Singer* — Al Jolson's historic line: "You ain't heard nothing yet"
- *Little Caesar* (1931) — Early gangster dialog shaping character
- *The Public Enemy* (1931)—James Cagney's iconic voice-driven performance
- *Singin' in the Rain* — Behind-the-scenes chaos of early sound shown through comedy

These clips help you see how sound shifted tone, character, and storytelling.

2. Try It Yourself — Sound Experiments

A. **The Microphone Trap:** Record a short scene using only one stationary microphone. Notice how limited movement changes your performance, the same challenge early actors faced.

B. **The Sync Challenge:** Film someone speaking, mute the audio, and try to match a new audio track to their lips. This tiny task shows why early filmmakers struggled to sync sound and image.

C. **Silent vs Sound Scene:** Shoot a scene twice, once silently and once with dialog. Compare which version feels more emotional, clearer, or more intense.

3. Sound Tech Simplified

A quick breakdown you can visualize while reading:

- **Sound-on-Disc:** Audio played on a separate record that tried to stay in sync with the film
- **Sound-on-Film:** Audio waves printed directly on the film strip, becoming the standard method
- **Why Syncing Was Hard:** Two machines, running in real time, with no digital tools

4. Spot the Difference

Compare:

- a silent acting scene (over-expressive but visual)
- an early sound scene (stiff, microphone-bound, awkward)
- a later sound film once technology improved

This helps you to see how acting evolved as technology matured.

Think about your favorite creators. How do they use sound? Voice? Music? Silence? Would they be as impactful in the silent era? Would you?

This short reflection can help teens see how the evolution of sound continues to shape their world today.

CHAPTER 3:

LIGHTS, COLOR, ACTION

"Here's looking at you, kid."
— Casablanca (1942)

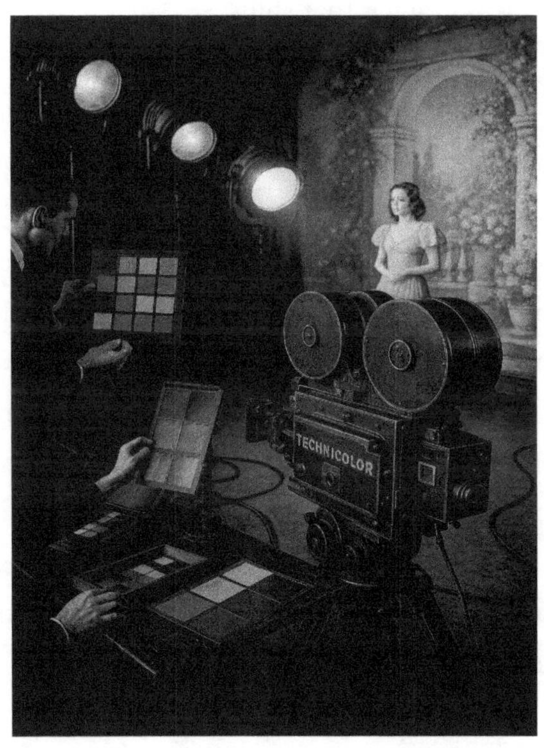

1939 → 1959

Imagine watching a world unfold in shades of grey. Not in a lifeless tone, just stripped down to form, shadow, and emotion. Black-and-white cinema had its own poetry. It trained audiences to notice details, to read expressions, and to follow movement with precision. But even in the height of that era, filmmakers knew something was missing. They could show you the world, but they couldn't show you how it felt.

Think about how different a sunset looks when it's filtered through your phone vs when you see it with your own eyes. One is an image. The other is an experience. Color doesn't just decorate a scene; it adds mood, temperature, and emotional weight.

Cinema was craving that shift.

Before color took over, filmmakers leaned hard into what they had. They used lighting like paintbrushes, shadows as storytelling tools, and contrast to build tension. For a while, it worked; audiences loved the clarity and drama of black-and-white stories, but as technology grew and filmmakers experimented, people started asking the same question: what would happen if movies didn't just speak… but glowed?

Color was a dream that kept knocking on cinema's door, long before Technicolor made it possible. Early attempts brought muted reds and strange greens, more like tinted memories than real hues. These experiments teased and hinted at a future where the screen could burst open.

That future wasn't far away.

Cinema had learned to move. Then it learned to speak. Now it was ready for its next evolution, which was learning how to live in full color.

TECHNICOLOR

1916 → 1932

The leap into color didn't happen through a single invention or a single lucky breakthrough. It arrived slowly, unevenly, like someone testing different brushes before painting the sky. Early filmmakers experimented with tinting entire scenes blue for night, red for fire, or amber for daylight, but those colors washed over everything like a filter instead of revealing true detail. They were beautiful in their own way, but they weren't the world.

The desire for real color kept growing, and that desire eventually found a name: Technicolor.

Technicolor's earliest versions were impressive on paper but difficult in practice. Their two-color system captured only red and green, leaving films looking dreamlike but incomplete. Skin tones appeared strange, landscapes felt limited, and costumes lost their depth. Yet filmmakers kept experimenting because even imperfect color offered a kind of magic.

These early attempts were stepping stones, proof that color could blend with storytelling instead of distracting from it. Audiences didn't just want colored frames; they wanted colored worlds.

The Three-Strip Revolution

Everything changed when Technicolor introduced its three-strip camera. Instead of capturing two colors, it recorded red, green, and blue separately, using three strips of film running through the camera at the same time. When combined, they produced colors that finally felt natural — vibrant, warm, and full of dimension.

There was a catch. The camera was huge, heavy, and loud. It required bright lights that overheated sets and exhausted actors. Technicians known as Technicolor consultants supervised every shot to ensure the colors met strict guidelines. But the result was undeniable: cinema finally had the palette it had been dreaming of.

How Color Became Emotion

The arrival of actual color didn't just change how films looked; it changed how stories were told. Directors used color to convey mood in ways black-and-white never could.

Soft pastels could paint innocence or nostalgia. Bold reds could signal danger or passion. Deep blues could set the tone for mystery or melancholy. Color became a narrative tool, guiding how audiences felt without a single line of dialog. So it became a new feature, a new form of storytelling, and a few films proved just how powerful it could be. These weren't the first color films ever made, but they were the ones that made audiences sit forward, widen their eyes, and realize they were witnessing a turning point. They didn't treat color as decoration. They treated it as meaning.

The Wizard of Oz

Nothing in cinema history captures the arrival of color better than the moment Dorothy opens the door of her small Kansas home. Inside the house, everything is brown and muted, familiar and grounded. Once she steps into Oz, the world explodes into vibrant color. It feels like someone took a black-and-white dream and peeled it open.

Audiences in 1939 felt the shift physically, the same way people today feel their stomach drop during a dramatic camera reveal, or a game-changing CGI shot. The moment wasn't just visual, it was emotional. Oz didn't just look different. It *felt* different. Color turned the world into a fantasy that was suddenly believable.

This single transition taught filmmakers that color could be used to separate worlds, shift tone, and guide feeling without a single word of explanation.

Gone with the Wind

Where *The Wizard of Oz* used color to build fantasy, *Gone with the Wind* used it to build grandeur. Sweeping landscapes, burning cities, elegant costumes, and dramatic lighting created a sense of scale that black-and-white simply couldn't match.

One of the most iconic scenes — Atlanta burning — is unforgettable because of how the reds and oranges take over the frame. The color itself carries the tension and emotional weight. It creates an atmosphere without needing music or dialog to explain it. This film proved that color could elevate scale and transform a story into an experience.

Snow White and the Seven Dwarfs

Disney's *Snow White* (1937) was the first full-length cel-animated feature, and its use of Technicolor created a world that felt warm, inviting, and artistically unified. Every shade was intentional. Every background painted with care. The use of color in animation didn't just make the film beautiful; it set the standard for decades of animated storytelling. Color helped animators guide emotion, highlight danger, build magic, and create visual rhythm. Scenes became more musical because the palette worked like a score.

These movies succeeded because they understood why color mattered. They treated every hue as emotion, every contrast as tension, and every splash of color as a part of the story's heartbeat. Once these films revealed how powerful a thoughtful palette could be, directors and studios everywhere realized that cinema had entered a new era in which the screen wasn't just a window, but a canvas waiting to be painted.

THE RISE OF THE STUDIO SYSTEM

When color began reshaping the look of movies, something just as powerful was reshaping the way movies were made. Filmmaking stopped feeling like a handful of dreamers experimenting in warehouses, and started operating more like a fully trained machine. The moment studios realized that movies could pull in massive audiences across the country, they built an industry designed to deliver films with the same consistency and force as any major business.

Five major companies rose to the top:

1. MGM
2. Warner Bros
3. Paramount
4. Fox
5. RKO

They created a system where nearly everything happened under one roof. A studio didn't just make films. It owned theaters, controlled distribution, trained talent, and kept a roster of stars under contract. Actors were tied to long-term deals that shaped their careers, their public image, and their future.

Directors, writers, and designers worked within these studios as part of a stable creative workforce. Sets were built in huge backlots that held entire miniature cities. Costumes were stored in warehouses the size of supermarkets. Studio schedules ran with military precision. It wasn't unusual for an actor to finish one scene, walk across the lot, and jump straight into another character for a completely different film.

The system ran fast, polished, and tightly controlled, producing movies at a pace that shaped what the world expected from Hollywood.

This era introduced the idea of star power. Studios didn't wait for audiences to discover actors naturally. They crafted stars the way music labels cultivate artists today. Publicists managed how they spoke, dressed and appeared in magazines. Stylists shaped their looks. Acting coaches strengthened their screen presence. Image was everything.

Someone like Judy Garland didn't just rise because she was talented. She rose because a studio invested in her voice, her persona, and her visibility. Clark Gable arrived with the full weight of MGM behind him. Katharine Hepburn built her reputation through a mix of independence and star image carefully shaped by her studio. This was marketing; the art of creating cinematic icons.

Furthermore, since studios held so much power, they began favoring stories that fit their strengths.

- MGM leaned into glamorous musicals.
- Warner Bros thrived on gritty crime dramas.
- Paramount built sharp comedies.
- Fox specialized in swashbuckling adventures.
- RKO shaped the foundations of atmospheric thrillers.

Genres weren't just creative categories; they were business strategies, and because audiences knew what each studio did best, the system created a rhythm, a cinematic ecosystem where every release carried an identity.

Scroll through modern entertainment, and you'll see echoes of this system everywhere:

- Agencies shaping influencers.
- Labels developing artists.
- Streaming platforms curating specific identities.

The studio system was the blueprint for creative industries today. When this era reached its peak, Hollywood was a global machine, polished and powerful, shaping culture, storytelling, and stardom on a scale the world had never seen. Furthermore, certain stars rose within that era:

Judy Garland

A voice that could break your heart and stitch it back together in the same breath. Her emotional honesty drew audiences in, especially in *The Wizard of Oz*, where her blend of vulnerability and strength set a new standard for musical storytelling.

Clark Gable

Confident, charismatic, and unshakably composed. Known best for *Gone with the Wind*, he became the blueprint for the stylish Hollywood leading man.

Katharine Hepburn

Sharp, independent, and unwavering. Her performances carried a clarity and strength that redefined the image of a Hollywood heroine.

James Stewart

The everyman with a warm presence. His sincerity made him relatable, grounding dramas and thrillers alike with natural charm.

Humphrey Bogart

Cool, understated intensity. Films like *Casablanca* and *The Maltese Falcon* showed how his quiet confidence could guide an entire story.

Ingrid Bergman

Graceful, luminous, and emotionally rich. She brought depth to roles that demanded both vulnerability and quiet power.

Vivien Leigh

Magnetic and unpredictable. Her performance in *Gone with the Wind* delivered both elegance and fire, capturing audiences instantly.

Fred Astaire & Ginger Rogers

Together, they turned dance into storytelling. Their movement, rhythm, and chemistry transformed musicals into works of elegance and joy.

Gene Kelly

Dynamic and athletic. His energy in *Singin' in the Rain* reshaped the musical genre through physical expression and vibrant choreography.

Dorothy Dandridge

A groundbreaking presence. Her talent and poise opened doors for future performers of color while proving that stardom had no single blueprint.

These stars carried different strengths: voice, movement, charisma, and emotional range, but together they built the myth of Hollywood glamor. They became part of a larger tapestry of style, personality, and presence that made the Golden Age feel larger than life. Their influence still shows up today in performers who draw from their grace, confidence and emotional clarity. The era shaped how we think about fame, how we imagine heroes and how we define a cinematic icon.

THE HAYS CODE AND HOLLYWOOD'S GLOBAL GLOW

1930 → 1968

Hollywood's Golden Age glowed brightly on screen, but behind the scenes, it ran under a strict rulebook that shaped nearly every story produced during this era. As films grew more popular and reached wider audiences, studio leaders and political voices pushed for a set of boundaries that would keep movies within a specific moral framework. The result was a code of conduct that influenced not just how stories were told, but what stories could even exist.

The Hays Code

The Motion Picture Production Code, often called the Hays Code, stepped in during the 1930s with clear goals: protect audiences, safeguard morality, and keep Hollywood's image polished. Instead of letting studios explore every kind of theme freely, the code outlined what could appear on screen.

1. Romance had to feel respectful rather than suggestive.
2. Crime couldn't be rewarded. Dialog avoided profanity.
3. Violence stayed controlled.
4. Characters weren't allowed to challenge certain moral expectations.

Filmmakers adjusted quickly. Instead of pushing against the rules, they began using implication, symbolism, and timing to express ideas indirectly. A lingering glance held more weight than a physical kiss. Sharp dialog replaced explicit moments. Tension grew through pacing rather than shock.

Restrictions created a new kind of creativity.

- Directors found ways to communicate emotion and conflict through subtlety.
- Writers learned to craft scenes that played out beneath the surface.
- Audiences became sharper viewers because they had to read between the lines.

As American studios mastered their formula of glamor, romance, color, and tight storytelling, their films spread across continents. In many countries, Hollywood movies became a window into another world. Audiences watched elegant costumes, polished acting, and smooth dialog, shaping ideas of fashion, lifestyle, and modern identity.

Hollywood's consistency made its films easy to export. Studios produced movies with clear genres, recognizable stars, and high production value, which made international audiences feel instantly familiar with American cinema. Some countries embraced the influence and built theaters that mirrored Hollywood's presentation. Others blended the American style with their own traditions, shaping hybrid film cultures.

The studio system also laid the foundation for global fandom. International audiences recognized the same stars, followed the same films, and admired the same performances.

Posters traveled, magazines featured Hollywood faces, and moviegoers across the world connected through a shared cinematic language.

When the Golden Age reached full force, Hollywood had become more than a film industry. It was a cultural landmark. The Hays Code shaped the tone of stories, while Hollywood's reach influenced how people around the world viewed movies, identity, and storytelling.

The glow of this era didn't stay locked in America. It drifted into global cinema, influencing genres, visual style, and the idea of stardom for generations.

As color deepened and emotion intensified, studios refined their storytelling, and a new wave of international film movements was already forming, ready to challenge Hollywood's dominance and reshape the world's understanding of cinema once again.

WHEN CINEMA LEARNED TO SHINE

Cinema entered the Golden Age with sound in its lungs and color in its bloodstream, but what truly defined this era wasn't the technology; it was the confidence. Hollywood learned how to build worlds with precision, craft stars with intention, and shape stories with a clarity that reached beyond borders. Films carried a glow that audiences recognized instantly, a blend of rich color, polished performance, and steady craftsmanship that made moviegoing feel like an experience rather than a pastime.

The Hays Code guided the tone from behind the curtain, setting boundaries that pushed filmmakers toward subtlety and suggestion, while the global reach of Hollywood turned its stars and stories into shared cultural reference points. People across continents looked to the same screens, followed the same faces, and imagined themselves inside the same dreams.

This era didn't last forever, but its impact did. It laid the foundation for modern stardom, shaped visual language, and established Hollywood as a creative force the world couldn't ignore. And as the Golden Age reached its peak, new ideas were gathering in the distance, ideas that would introduce global movements, shift artistic priorities and challenge Hollywood's dominance.

The spotlight was bright, but cinema was preparing to evolve again.

The Golden Age lives in the collective memory of cinema because it marked a time when every aspect of filmmaking seemed to rise at once. As you think back on this chapter, consider how sound, color, performance, and storytelling shaped the films you watch today. Think about how much of modern visual culture, from acting styles to lighting choices to global fandom, carries echoes from this era.

Ask yourself a few questions as you move into the next chapter:

- Which Golden Age films or stars still influence the kind of content you enjoy now?
- How does color shape your emotional response to a story?

- What stands out more — the rules that held filmmakers back or the creativity they discovered because of those boundaries?

Hold these questions lightly. They're a reminder that cinema is a conversation across time, and you're part of it now.

CHAPTER 4

REBELS, RULE-BREAKERS & WORLD CHANGERS

"You talkin' to me?"
— Taxi Driver (1976)

1959 → 1979

Color reshaped the screen, studios perfected their formulas, and Hollywood's Golden Age glowed with a confidence that felt untouchable. Stars shimmered with polish, stories moved with rhythm, and the dream factory ran with a precision that looked impossible to challenge. Yet while audiences were dazzled by sweeping Technicolor worlds and velvet-curtained premieres, something entirely different was stirring beneath the surface.

A new generation was growing up with their sleeves rolled up, music louder, hearts heavier, and tempers shorter. The world outside the theater was shifting very fast. Teenagers were discovering their identities amid cultural earthquakes. Countries were rebuilding, reinventing, and some even resisting. Global voices were sharpening in the shadows of polished backlots. Filmmakers looked around at the glamorous machine Hollywood had built and felt a spark in their chest, saying, *What if stories could breathe differently? What if cameras could move differently? What if cinema could break its own rules?*

The glow of the Golden Age reached every corner of the world, but the reflections didn't all look the same. In some cities, directors picked up cameras like they were weapons. In others, young artists treated film like a confession, a form of rebellion, poetry, or protest. Some people found themselves in cheap drive-ins and packed theaters, hungry for stories that matched the fire in their own lives. And across oceans, entire nations began shaping cinematic identities that felt raw and electric, carried by real streets, real people, real struggle, real emotion.

The screen was about to crack open, not with color this time, but with courage.

This was the moment when cinema stopped whispering and started pushing back. When the world's storytellers crossed a line and didn't bother looking behind them. When youth culture, global movements, and artistic rebellion collided with the force of a supernova.

Hollywood had given the world a dream. Now the world was ready to dream on its own terms.

Welcome to the era where film got bolder, rougher, deeper, stranger, and braver; an era where directors didn't wait for permission and audiences didn't want perfection. The camera finally learned to run wild, and every frame carried the pulse of a world in revolution.

TEEN REBELS & DRIVE-INS

As the Golden Age lights began to cool, a different kind of energy was rumbling beneath the surface, not from studios or producers, but from the youth of the world. Teenagers were no longer background characters in society. They were becoming a force, a mood, a culture with its own heartbeat. Their fashion changed, their music shifted, their voices sharpened, and their hunger for something real began to echo through the streets.

You could feel it in the way young people moved; louder radios, faster cars, sharper attitudes. There was a restlessness in the air, a feeling that the world adults had built wasn't built for them. And in that tension, cinema found a new pulse.

Screens lit up with stories about young people trying to figure themselves out in a world that didn't seem to understand them. And when James Dean stepped into frame with that impossible mix of rebellion and vulnerability, teenagers finally saw themselves reflected with all the rawness they carried inside. Films like '*Rebel Without a Cause*' captured the quiet storms building inside a generation that felt caught between expectation and desire.

However, the revolution wasn't only happening on the screen; it was happening in the places where movies were watched. Drive-ins began popping up across America, glowing like neon playgrounds for teens who needed escape, privacy, romance, or just somewhere to breathe. These spaces weren't polished or glamorous. They were messy, loud, alive, a cultural stage where engines hummed like nervous hearts and the night sky became an open ceiling for stories.

Cars lined up facing giant screens that rose from the darkness like glowing monuments. Kids shared milkshakes, argued over plots, laughed too loudly, and sometimes never even made it past the first act because the real drama was happening inside the car. Drive-ins turned moviegoing into a social ritual, a teenage rite of passage where freedom tasted like popcorn and possibility.

Studios noticed this and observed what teens were drawn to: danger, romance, speed, rebellion, and built films that matched the pulse. Motorcycle gangs roaring into towns. Hot-rod heroes racing toward trouble. Rock 'n' roll shaking the speakers while onscreen characters broke rules adults had spent decades trying to reinforce. Teenagers weren't just audiences anymore; they were the compass.

With every passing year, the screen leaned a little closer to them. Stories grew wilder. Plots sharpened. Soundtracks thumped with the rhythm of restless youth. Cinema wasn't simply reflecting culture; it was accelerating it, capturing the electricity of a generation discovering its own voice in real time.

This shift cracked the door open for all the rule-breaking movements that would follow. Directors around the world were watching, taking notes, and feeling empowered to push further and let films breathe, look, and move differently.

The young had taken over the drive-ins, and soon, they'd take over the camera.

THE FRENCH NEW WAVE

Across the ocean, a different spark was catching fire: Young filmmakers in France were watching the polished, neatly packaged movies coming out of Hollywood and felt something tightening in their chest. The world around them was messy, alive, unpredictable. Why should cinema feel any different?

So they picked up lightweight cameras, stepped into real streets, and let the world become their set. No giant studios, no rigid rules, no polished glamor. Just raw life, captured as it unfolded. And suddenly, film didn't feel like a distant dream anymore.

The movement that followed hit like a jolt to the global system (Maio, 2015). Jean-Luc Godard, François Truffaut, Agnès Varda, and Jacques Rivette are names that carried the energy of young rebels with something urgent to say. They spoke through jump cuts, handheld shots, stolen locations, broken structure, and characters who felt more like people you might pass on the street than scripted heroes.

Breathless tore through cinema like a storm: cuts that chopped time, characters who spoke directly to the audience, scenes that wandered with intention, as if the movie itself was thinking out loud. *The 400 Blows* traced childhood with a tenderness that felt painfully real, shot in alleys, classrooms, cramped apartments; the real Paris, not the postcard version.

What made this wave unforgettable wasn't the technique but the attitude.

These directors treated the camera like a friend they trusted with their secrets. They filmed conversations the way people actually talk: messy, overlapping, drifting from humor to heartbreak. They let silence stay when it needed to stay. They broke the neat little boxes previous generations spent decades building and replaced them with movement that felt spontaneous, personal, alive.

The world was watching, and whether audiences understood every choice or not, they felt the freedom in every frame. The French New Wave shaped modern expression. The jump cuts you see in vlogs, the shaky handheld style in indie films, the meta humor in shows that wink at the audience, traces of this movement ripple through everything.

It wasn't rebellion for rebellion's sake. It was young creators telling the world, *We're here now, and this is how we see it.* Once that door opened, it didn't close.

ITALIAN NEOREALISM

While French filmmakers were breaking form with style and bravado, Italy was carving out an entirely different cinematic heartbeat, one built from rubble, resilience, and the quiet strength of ordinary people. The country was recovering from war, its cities scarred, its families fractured, its economy shaken to the core. Glamor had no place in the streets of Rome or Naples. Life was raw, unpredictable, and achingly human. Filmmakers didn't look away. They walked straight into it (Heckmann, 2019).

Italian Neorealism rose from that landscape like a voice too honest to ignore. Directors stepped out of the studios and into the real world, letting cracked sidewalks, crowded markets, broken walls, and open skies become their sets. Instead of polished movie stars, they cast non-actors like parents, laborers, and children; people whose lives carried the weight and truth the camera was hungry for.

Films like *Bicycle Thieves* held up a mirror to everyday struggles with a tenderness that made audiences feel as though they were walking beside the characters. A father searching for his stolen bike wasn't just a plot; it was a symbol of dignity, survival, and the fragile threads families cling to. *Rome, Open City* captured the streets with a rawness that felt almost documentary, its scenes shaped by real fear, real resistance, real courage.

Neorealism chased honesty. The camera followed people in their natural rhythm: long walks across crowded cities, quiet conversations in cramped kitchens, moments of laughter, frustration, hope, and heartbreak. Lighting was natural because life provided its own shadows. Dialog felt unpolished because emotions rarely come out clean. Everything breathed with the truth of lived experience.

What made this movement unforgettable was its empathy. These films carried the pulse of a nation trying to rebuild itself from the inside out. They treated ordinary lives with the gravity of epic stories, reminding the world that heroism isn't always loud; sometimes it's a parent searching for work, a child navigating a harsh city, a community holding each other up through impossible days.

Modern creators still chase the spirit Neorealism captured. You can see its fingerprints in indie films shot on real streets, in lo-fi YouTube documentaries, in stories that unfold with unfiltered vulnerability. Whenever a filmmaker chooses truth over gloss, connection over perfection, the echo of Neorealism is right there, breathing beneath the frame.

Italy showed the world that cinema doesn't always need polish to be powerful. Sometimes it just needs courage, compassion, and a lens pointed at the heart of real life.

JAPANESE CINEMA UNLEASHED

Meanwhile, Japan's cinematic roar began with discipline, rhythm, and a deep respect for the silence between moments. While the West pushed toward rebellion through chaos, Japan carved its revolution through precision; the kind of intentionality that makes every frame feel like a brushstroke.

Akira Kurosawa led the charge with a vision that moved like weather: sweeping when it needed force, quiet when it needed weight, always intentional. His stories unfolded with the pulse of ancient myths and the urgency of modern life. *Seven Samurai* gathered characters the way storms gather clouds; slowly, inevitably, with a pressure that builds until something unforgettable erupts. That film didn't just tell a story, it created a template for how teams assemble, how tension breathes, how action moves with purpose.

Kurosawa's editing carried its own signature. His "axial cuts" shifted perspective like a heartbeat, pulling viewers closer, then dropping them back into the scene. His "wipe transitions" sliced through time with the decisiveness of a sword. Hollywood studied those choices like sacred text.

Decades later, *Star Wars* borrowed the very same wipes, proving how Japanese cinema quietly reshaped global storytelling.

Yet Japan's impact wasn't carried only by samurai tales. Yasujiro Ozu moved in the opposite direction: stillness, minimalism, emotional clarity. His camera sat low, almost at eye level when sitting on a tatami mat, inviting viewers into the quiet spaces families rarely speak about. Films like *Tokyo Story* unfolded, gently revealing truths about aging, distance, love, and the quiet ache of changing times.

Where Kurosawa used storms, Ozu used silence.

Then came the thunder.

In 1954, a giant emerged from the ocean and changed the world forever. *Godzilla* stomped into theaters carrying more than destruction. Beneath the rubble and screams was a nation processing trauma — the memory of Hiroshima and Nagasaki echoing through every roar. The creature wasn't just a monster; it was a metaphor, a wound, a warning shaped into cinematic myth.

Kaiju films erupted from that moment, blending spectacle with symbolism. Crowds packed theaters not only for the chaos, but for the catharsis. And across the world, audiences absorbed a new kind of fantasy that carried truth under its scales.

Japan's influence didn't stop with samurai, family dramas, or monsters the size of cities. Seeds were being planted for a movement that would blossom into a global phenomenon. Early animated experiments, inventive storytelling, and bold visual style were paving the way for what would eventually become anime's rise.

Everything Japan touched, from composition to editing to mythmaking, rippled outward. Hollywood blockbusters adopted its pacing. Global directors borrowed its emotional clarity. Fans across continents fell in love with kaiju, samurai, family dramas, and animated worlds that felt more alive than reality.

Japanese cinema didn't just join the global conversation. It shifted it, proving that the most powerful stories don't always shout. Sometimes they cut, roar, or whisper their way into history.

WOMEN WHO CALLED THE SHOTS

While the world's film movements were erupting with rebellion, innovation, and raw new voices, another revolution was unfolding quietly — one carried by women who refused to wait for permission. The system wasn't built for them, the doors weren't open for them, and the spotlight rarely turned their way, but they stepped behind the camera anyway, carving space where none existed.

Ida Lupino stood at the forefront, sharp-eyed and unshakable. She started as an actress, navigating the studio system with the grace expected of Hollywood stars, but the moment she stepped behind the camera, her voice sharpened. Lupino told stories the industry avoided, stories about working-class struggle, trauma, and the complex inner worlds women carried long before the world cared to listen. Her sets ran with discipline, her shots carried emotional precision, and her filmmaking became a quiet rebellion wrapped in craft (Barson, 2025).

Shirley Clarke approached cinema with a different kind of electricity. She gravitated toward the rhythms of the streets: jazz clubs, cramped apartments, voices on the margins. Clarke's films felt like pulse readings — jittery, intimate, alive. She moved through the documentary and experimental scenes with the confidence of someone who understood that truth didn't need polishing to hit hard. Her work cracked open conversations about identity, race, youth culture, and the weight of being unseen (Satchell-Baeza, 2019).

Agnès Varda brought poetry into the revolution. Often called the "grandmother of the New Wave," she shaped the movement from its roots with a voice entirely her own. Her films blended documentary honesty with fictional grace, capturing tiny human gestures with the same reverence given to epic stories. Varda had a gift for revealing the soul inside ordinary life, a glimmer in the eye, a pause in a sentence, a hand resting on a windowsill, and letting those moments carry entire worlds.

These women pushed against the system with clarity. Furthermore, they directed with intention, framed humanity with their own perspective, and carried stories that had been overlooked, dismissed, or buried beneath the noise of a male-dominated industry.

What they created was space for new ways of seeing. Space for voices long unheard. Space for the next generation to step into without apology.

Modern filmmakers study their work because their fingerprints are everywhere. You see Lupino in character-driven dramas that explore private pain with honesty. You see Clarke in gritty street-level storytelling and documentary hybrids. You see Varda in every filmmaker who uses quiet observation as a form of power.

These women didn't wait to be invited onto the stage. They built their own and lit it themselves.

BLACK CINEMA & BLAXPLOITATION

Long before Hollywood was ready to embrace Black stories, Black filmmakers were already building their own cinematic worlds — stories shaped by resilience, pride, survival, joy, and the fire of communities determined to see themselves on screen. These films didn't wait for mainstream approval. They grew from necessity, from voices that refused to be silent, and from audiences hungry for reflections that felt true.

Oscar Micheaux was one of the earliest architects of this movement. Working outside the studio system, he wrote, produced, and directed films that confronted racial injustice head-on. His characters pushed against the boundaries America placed around them, and his stories exposed truths the mainstream industry avoided. Micheaux didn't just create films — he created a blueprint for independent Black cinema, proving that vision mattered more than permission.

As decades passed and social tides shifted, new waves of Black filmmakers emerged, each bringing their own perspective. By the early 1970s, a cultural earthquake was building. Black audiences were tired of being relegated to the background in Hollywood stories. They wanted leads who looked like them, spoke like them, carried the swagger, the strength, the vulnerability, and the complexity they saw in their communities. The response became one of the most influential and controversial movements in film history: ***'Blaxploitation' (*Davis, 2021).

The word itself blended two ideas: Black empowerment and Hollywood's tendency to exploit trends. But inside this tension came a surge of bold, unapologetic films that electrified audiences. Heroes walked through danger with style sharp enough to cut glass. Heroines carried both beauty and fury, commanding the screen with a presence that couldn't be dimmed.

Shaft swaggered onto screens with a theme song that hit like an anthem. *Super Fly* pulsed with attitude and ambition. And Pam Grier, fierce, iconic, and unforgettable, redefined what a female action lead could be, playing characters who survived, fought back, and refused to be minimized.

These films were loud, stylish, rebellious, and full of cultural fire. They mixed action with soul, politics with personality, danger with rhythm. For the first time, Black audiences saw themselves not as sidekicks or stereotypes, but as the center of the story that was complex, powerful, flawed, and human.

Yet the movement's impact ran deeper than the screen. Blaxploitation shaped fashion, music, and attitude. Funk and soul blasted from theater speakers and spilled into the streets. Leather jackets, wide-lapel suits, afros, and boots became symbols of pride. These films turned neighborhoods into cinematic battlegrounds and sanctuaries, celebrating identity at a scale Hollywood had never acknowledged.

But within the celebration came conversation. Some praised the movement for creating heroes who finally stood tall. Others questioned the risks of Hollywood simplifying Black identity for profit. What mattered most was that these films cracked open space — space for bigger conversations, bolder voices, and a new generation of storytellers.

From the roots Micheaux planted to the fire Blaxploitation lit, Black cinema shifted the landscape. It paved the way for directors like Spike Lee, Ava DuVernay, Ryan Coogler, Jordan Peele, Gina Prince-Bythewood, and so many others who would carry forward stories filled with depth, nuance, and power.

Black cinema didn't ask to be included in Hollywood's narrative. It made its own, and the world is still catching up.

WHEN CINEMA FOUND ITS COURAGE

Every movement in this chapter carried a spark, some subtle, some explosive, but all of them pushed cinema into a bolder shape. Youth culture cracked open the door. French rebels shattered the frame. Italian storytellers grounded film in lived truth. Japan elevated precision into poetry and myth. Women carved space where none was offered. Black filmmakers built worlds of resilience and identity that reshaped generations.

Together, they formed a constellation of voices that refused to be silent. Cinema stopped behaving like a system and began reflecting a living, breathing reflection of a changing world.

This era didn't move in straight lines or clean categories. It moved as life does through resistance, reinvention, and the courage to chase stories that mattered. And every filmmaker who dared to step outside the expected left a trail for others to follow.

The screen had become a mirror, a megaphone, and sometimes a fist raised in the air. The world changed, and cinema changed with it.

Here's a playful, creative mix of prompts, suggestions, and cinematic drills for you to explore, compare, and think with, nothing overwhelming, just sparks you can follow in your own time.

1. The "Spot the DNA" Challenge

Watch one modern film or series you love, and look for the ghosts of earlier movements:

- A jump cut that feels like Godard.
- A quiet emotional beat straight out of Ozu.
- A gritty street scene echoing Italian Neorealism.
- A fierce, stylish entrance that channels Blaxploitation swagger.
- A poetic detail that feels like something Varda would notice.

You'll start seeing connections everywhere.

2. Compare These Pairings

Watch (or look up scenes from) these film duos and feel how the past flows into the present:

- **Blaxploitation → Modern Parallel**
  Shaft (1971) → Black Panther (2018)
- **Italian Neorealism → Modern Realism**
  Bicycle Thieves (1948) → The Florida Project (2017)
- **French New Wave → Meta Storytelling**
  Breathless (1960) → Frances Ha (2012)
- **Japanese Cinema → Global Action DNA**
  Seven Samurai (1954) → The Magnificent Seven (2016)
- **Women Who Called the Shots → Modern Echo**
  Cléo from 5 to 7 (1962) → Portrait of a Lady on Fire (2019)

You don't need to watch all of them. Even clips reveal how ideas travel across decades.

3. A Quick Dive Into the Legends

Pick any one person from this chapter and spend five minutes searching their work:

- Ida Lupino
- Agnès Varda
- Oscar Micheaux
- Pam Grier
- Akira Kurosawa
- Shirley Clarke
- François Truffaut
- Ozu Yasujiro
- Sergio Leone

Just five minutes and you'll be surprised how fast their worlds pull you in.

4. The "What If" Remix

Imagine your favorite modern movie remade by a different movement from this chapter:

- A superhero film shot like Italian Neorealism.
- A rom-com directed with French New Wave freedom.
- A thriller edited with Kurosawa's wipe transitions.
- A coming-of-age story told with Varda's tenderness.
- An action film with Blaxploitation attitude.

This exercise trains your "cinematic imagination" — the same muscle directors use.

5. Three Films to Watch When You're Ready

- **Do the Right Thing** — A direct descendant of the voices in this chapter.
- **Princess Mononoke** — The spirit of Japanese cinema in full mythic force.
- **The 400 Blows** — Pure New Wave electricity.

Take your time. Watch whenever curiosity taps you on the shoulder.

Essentially, cinema grew teeth, wings, courage, and soul during this era because people chose to create from truth, not permission. If you carry anything from this journey, let it be this:

Every era of film was built by someone who decided the old rules weren't enough for the stories they had inside them.

And you've got that spark too.

CHAPTER 5:

THE SUMMER BLOCKBUSTER

"May the Force be with you."
— Star Wars (1977)

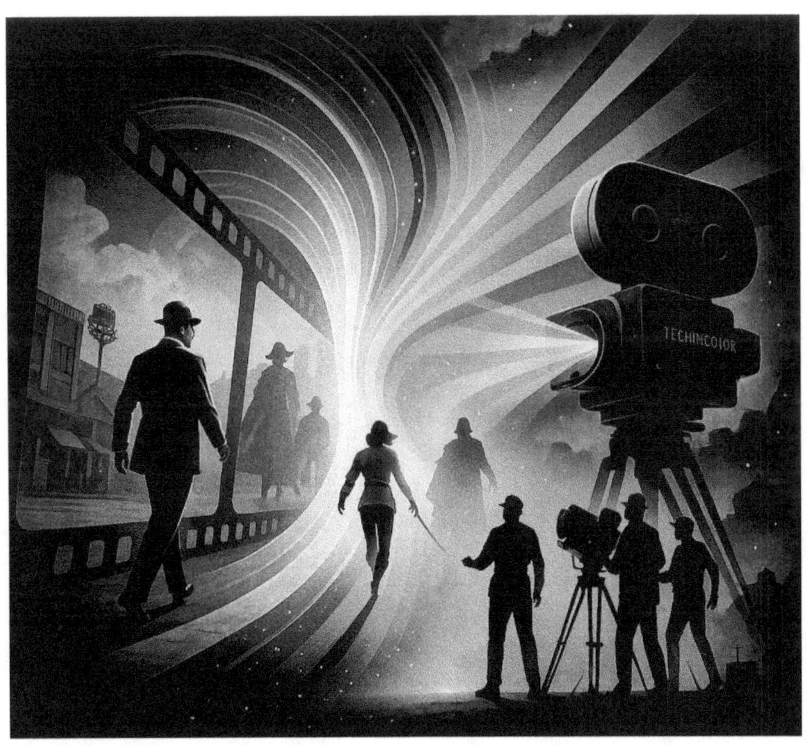

It started with a ripple. A quiet thrill in the air. A rumor that a movie wasn't just *good*, it was something you had to experience before anyone spoiled a single frame. Then the ripple turned into a wave, and suddenly crowds weren't just buying tickets… they were lining up around the block days before release, some with sleeping bags and snacks all for bragging rights. The movie wasn't even out yet, and it already felt like an event.

This was the moment cinema learned how to roar.

The 1970s cracked open a new kind of energy, stories no longer content to sit politely on the screen. They wanted to swallow the room, shake the floorboards, and send people stumbling out of the theater breathless. Films grew teeth and scale and spectacle, and audiences followed like they were answering a call.

Jaws struck first.

A shark you barely saw. A feeling you never forgot. The ocean suddenly felt bigger, darker, closer. People stepped out of theaters and refused to go near water for the rest of the summer. It wasn't fear alone, it was awe. A movie had reached into real life and rearranged it.

Then came *Star Wars*, and the world tilted on its axis.

A galaxy flashed across the screen with a confidence so bold it felt like the movie had been waiting for us, not the other way around. Lightsabers humming like ancient myths made modern. Spaceships roaring like mechanical beasts. Music swelling like destiny. Entire universes bursting open in seconds.

People didn't just watch Star Wars, they joined it.

Theaters overflowed as fans returned again and again, pulling friends along as if it was a pilgrimage. Lines wrapped corners, then blocks, then entire city streets. Merchandising exploded. Posters, toys, t-shirts, lunchboxes, soundtracks, suddenly your favorite movie wasn't something you left at the theater. You carried it with you.

A new blueprint was born: the blockbuster. Studios realized something powerful: if a movie hit the right nerve, it could take over the summer, dominate conversations, and ultimately, take over the world.

The blockbuster became a ritual. Midnight screenings. Fan theories whispered in long lines. Theme songs blasting from car radios. People choosing sides, quoting scenes, and memorizing dialog. Movies became events that stitched people together. Everything that followed, every franchise, every mega-sequel, every cinematic universe traces its pulse back to these first massive tremors. The era when movies stopped waiting for audiences and started pulling them in like gravity.

Once the blockbuster arrived, cinema would never be quiet again.

PRACTICAL EFFECTS FTW

Before computers took over the heavy lifting, movie magic was built by hand; sparks flying in workshops, glue on fingertips, paint on denim aprons, and entire teams huddled over miniature cities like giant kids building the world's coolest science projects. Special effects were crafted, engineered, sculpted, tested, broken, rebuilt, and pushed into greatness by imagination that refused limits.

The shift began with a studio in a warehouse: Industrial Light & Magic. A team of young artists, model makers, tinkerers, math wizards, and dreamers gathered with a single purpose: to bring Star Wars to life. And their approach stemmed from curiosity.

Model ships soared through galaxies built from painted glass and optical tricks. Cameras raced along motion-controlled tracks to give tiny ships the illusion of massive speed. Everyday objects became pieces of star destroyers. Car parts, plastics, wires, toy pieces, all transformed into the bones of an empire.

Nothing about it felt digital at the time. It was more physical rather. When the Millennium Falcon banked left or the X-wings dove into the Death Star trench, the movements carried weight because the models actually existed. Light hit their surfaces. Shadows wrapped around them. Every explosion sent real sparks flying.

Then came the creature makers. On the other side of the sci-fi universe, *E.T.* stepped into the world as an animatronic miracle layered with personality. Beneath the wrinkled skin was a complex blend of motors, hydraulics, wires, and puppeteers who breathed life into every tilt of the head and every flicker of emotion.

When Elliott touched E.T.'s glowing heart, audiences felt a connection rooted in something real: rubber, steel, mechanics, and intention all working together to create empathy.

Puppets blinked as miniatures trembled under simulated wind, creatures roared through layers of sound crafted from animals and machinery, fog machines hissed across the room, wires tugged at limbs, and artists kept experimenting until fantasy finally felt tangible, and fans felt it.

When you watch those scenes today, the magic still holds. Practical effects age like sculptures, imperfect at times, but honest in a way digital sheen can never replicate. There's soul in handmade worlds.

Behind every spaceship, creature, and glowing moment was a team solving problems with whatever they could get their hands on: coffee stirrers, cotton, motors pulled from broken appliances, sheets of metal hammered into shape. That mix of resourcefulness and imagination carried the same energy you see today in creators online who hack together props, costumes, or DIY short films, turning whatever they find into worlds that feel alive.

Practical effects didn't just change movies; they shaped how audiences dream. They proved that imagination doesn't need infinite budgets or digital perfection. It needs hands, teamwork, and the courage to try something no one has seen before. Furthermore, the worlds built in those workshops still echo through every modern blockbuster, every fan film, cosplay, creature design, and even a model-maker's desk. Some magic doesn't fade, it grows.

THE RISE OF THE SUPERFAN

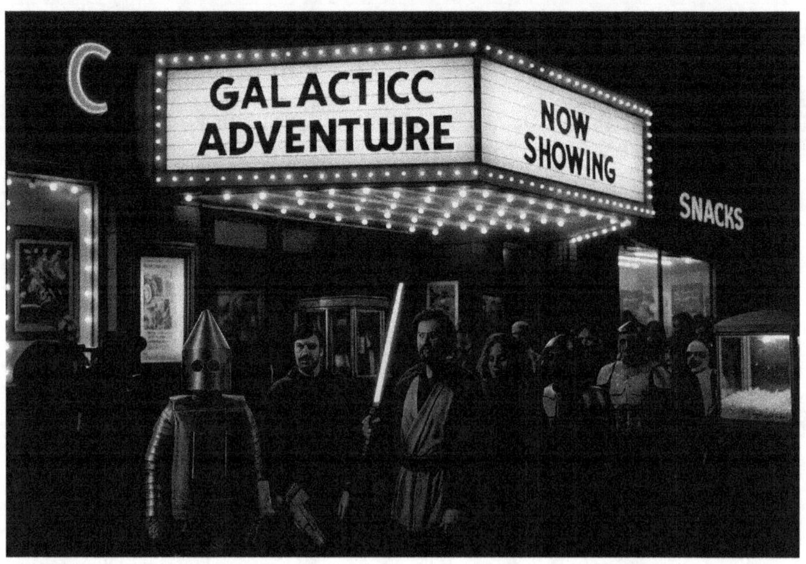

Long before social media, hashtags, and livestream reactions, something new began stirring inside packed theaters and buzzing convention halls. Audiences were no longer watching movies and walking away. They were carrying them home, wearing them, quoting them, building their identities around them. Stories became something people lived with, not for two hours, but for years.

The shift started with people camping outside theaters days before a premiere, swapping theories with strangers, and forming friendships in lines that wrapped around entire blocks. Fandom wasn't a word yet, but the feeling was unmistakable. Movies had turned into shared worlds that invited people in and refused to let them go.

Sci-fi conventions began sprouting up like small universes, places where you could walk through a doorway and suddenly be surrounded by people who spoke your language. Posters covered the walls. Merch tables stretched across rooms like treasure maps. Fans stood proudly in costumes they'd stitched, glued, painted, sculpted, and improvised from whatever they could afford.

Homemade stormtrooper armor cut from plastic sheets. Jedi robes sewn from thrift-store curtains. Phaser props built from flashlights and scraps of metal. Fans walked into convention halls carrying pieces of the stories they loved because people wanted to embody those worlds.

The moment a fan stepped into costume, the line between audience and storyteller blurred, and the universe expanded. The film left the screen and entered real life.

Studios noticed.

Merchandise exploded into a new kind of cultural currency. Action figures lined the shelves, and posters filled the bedrooms. Trading cards, lunchboxes, soundtracks, T-shirts, model kits, each item a tiny doorway back into the story. Kids acted out battles in their living rooms. Teens collected rare items like badges of honor. Adults built display shelves that looked like museum exhibits, and the studios learned something powerful: when people love a story deeply enough, they don't just watch it. They defend it, share it, celebrate it, and expand it.

Conventions grew into complete ecosystems, panels, screenings, Q&As, and fan films traded like secrets. People met their future best friends, collaborators, partners, or creative rivals. Some even launched careers after showing off costumes or fan-made props that caught the right eyes. The superfan wasn't someone with posters on the wall. The superfan was someone who felt the world inside the movie pulsing inside their own.

Every modern fandom, anime conventions, MCU stans, K-drama fanbases, gaming communities, online edit cultures, all trace their energy back to these first gatherings where people realized:

"I'm not alone in loving this."

That spark evolved into a movement that still defines pop culture today, and the next wave of cinema was already preparing to ride its coattails.

HIP-HOP, HORROR & NEW VOICES

The rise of the superfan didn't just build audiences. It cracked the door open for filmmakers who carried entire worlds inside them—worlds shaped by neighborhoods, music, migration, identity, danger, resilience, rhythm, and the kind of truth that doesn't fit neatly into Hollywood's polished mold. As blockbusters took over the multiplex, another movement grew in the shadows: storytellers who weren't chasing spectacle, but expression. And they certainly came in with fire.

The Beat of the Streets

Before Hollywood understood hip-hop, hip-hop had already become a cultural earthquake. It lived in parks, block parties, street corners, mixtapes, and neighborhoods that the mainstream rarely cared to look at until the energy became impossible to ignore.

When filmmakers began weaving hip-hop into cinema, the screen shifted. Suddenly, stories pulsed with bass, swagger, defiance, style, authenticity, and the poetry of lived experience. Directors like Spike Lee didn't soften their message for the sake of comfort. *Do the Right Thing* carried heat, anger, humor, and love all in the same frame, shot in colors so bold you could almost feel the temperature of the neighborhood rising. John Singleton, barely out of his teens, stepped forward with *Boyz n the Hood*, capturing family, fear, hope, and survival with the precision of someone who had lived every corner of the story.

These films represented a shift: communities finally seeing themselves projected with honesty.

Hip-hop brought:

- rhythm to dialog
- vibrance to color palettes
- grit to camera movement
- truth to character
- identity to soundtracks

It wasn't just background music, it was the heartbeat of something new.

Asia Turns Up the Heat — Horror, Action, and Style That Hit Different

Across the world, Asia was rewriting the rules again, quietly at first, then with a wave of films so bold they changed global cinema from the inside out.

Hong Kong exploded with kinetic action choreography. Filmmakers like John Woo reshaped the idea of movement, blending slow-motion gun battles, flying doves, double-handed pistols, and emotional faces streaked with sweat into a style so distinct it became a global influence.

Then J-horror rose with a different rhythm.

Films like *Ringu* and *Ju-On* approached fear through quiet precision, dread unfolding in slow breaths, silence stretching, shadows settling, and spirits emerging from stillness rather than force. This psychological tension shaped everything from *The Ring* remake to the pacing of modern horror.

At the center of this movement, Japanese creators layered emotional weight beneath their genre work, building an atmosphere that lingered long after the final scene.

Latino Stories Break Through

Latino filmmakers and storytellers had been shaping cinema for decades, but the late 80s and 90s gave rise to films that carried cultural truth with cinematic force. Directors like Robert Rodriguez hacked the system with DIY creativity. He famously shot *El Mariachi* for almost nothing, editing, scoring, and inventing on the fly. His success became proof that passion and vision outran budget.

Meanwhile, stories rooted in Chicano life, migration, identity, family bonds, and resistance found their way onto screens with deeper resonance. Films like *Stand and Deliver* showed heroism in quiet persistence. Others highlighted the weight of community, cultural pride, and the complexity of growing up between worlds. Essentially, Latino cinema was a rising pulse.

One Movement, Many Voices

What connected all these global breakthroughs wasn't genre or style. It was honesty. These filmmakers shaped their work from the ground they stood on, drawing from:

- their own rhythms
- their own fears
- their own humor
- their own cultural memory
- their own struggles and victories

Hip-hop brought truth. Asian cinema brought reinvention. Latino creators brought resilience.

And together, they reshaped the screen. Cinema wasn't just getting louder or more spectacular in this era. It was getting more human. More personal, more global, and more reflective of the world audiences lived in. A new wave of filmmakers had arrived, and their stories carried a heartbeat Hollywood could no longer ignore.

VIDEO STORES, VHS & AT-HOME MOVIE NIGHTS

The rise of new voices shook cinema from the inside, but something just as powerful was happening outside the theaters; a revolution sitting quietly in living rooms, backpacks, and rewinding machines that screeched like they were chewing on plastic. Suddenly, movies didn't belong to theaters anymore.

They belonged to everyone, and VHS turned the world into a personal cinema, one tape at a time.

There was nothing casual about walking into a video store. Whether it was the neon glow of Blockbuster or a small corner shop stacked with tapes, the moment you stepped inside, the whole place buzzed like a library full of alternate worlds. Aisles organized by action, romance, horror, comedy. Staff picks with handwritten notes. Faded posters taped to the walls. Fans arguing at the counter. Kids trying to convince their parents to let them rent one more movie. Suddenly, it became a ritual. This is where teens gained power over their movie choices. Instead of waiting for theaters or TV schedules, they could:

- choose what to watch
- pause and replay scenes
- explore genres freely
- discover cult classics tucked on dusty shelves
- watch movies at their own pace

The remote became a tool of education, rebellion, curiosity, and escape. Furthermore, VHS introduced a completely new behavior: rewatching and not a couple of times, but endlessly if need be.

Teens memorized lines, studied scenes, broke down choreography, copied poses, practiced impressions, debated endings, and rewound their favorite moments until the tape quality started to fade.

Some movies didn't become hits in theaters; they became legends on VHS. Cult classics grew because fans kept renting them:

- *The Terminator*
- *The Evil Dead*
- *The Breakfast Club*
- *Akira*
- *Heathers*
- *Clerks*

VHS turned quiet films into icons.

Home Movie Nights

Popcorn that somehow tasted better when poured into a giant mixing bowl. Blankets thrown across the floor like a soft battlefield. The TV humming in the corner, casting that warm blue glow across everyone's faces. Someone hogging the remote even though they promised they wouldn't. Someone else insisting they weren't scared… then screaming anyway.

This was the era when the living room became a universe.

Movie nights at home carried their own kind of magic. You didn't just *watch* movies, you lived inside them. Friends stretched across couches like sleepy dragons. Someone paused the film mid-plot twist because they "needed to say something real quick." Arguments broke out over theories. Jumpscares landed harder because the room felt too quiet. Comedy hit louder because everyone kept rewinding their favorite joke.

The home setup had its own rules:

- talk back to the screen like the characters can hear you
- pause mid-scene for snacks, debates, or dramatic effect
- build pillow fort seating if the couch is full
- laugh without strangers shushing you

- let reactions spill naturally; gasps, screams, tears, all of it

Those nights felt like sharing a story with the people who mattered. Inside jokes were born there. Lifelong favorites were discovered there. Some friendships even grew deeper because of what people confessed during a pause screen. Movies became memories and eventually turned personal.

However, before streaming, there were underground ecosystems. Friends copied movies for each other, and tapes were passed between classmates like contraband. Anime fans traded fansubs recorded over old tapes. Skaters passed around VHS edits of tricks. Horror fans shared obscure imports you couldn't find in any store.

So VHS didn't just give access, it created communities.

Ultimately, Video stores taught teens how to explore art on their own terms without algorithms, autoplay, or recommendations. All there was to it was curiosity.

VHS made film discovery feel like treasure hunting, digging through shelves until something strange, bold, or intriguing caught your eye. This era made movie lovers out of a whole generation because it handed them the remote and said:

"Go ahead. Choose your world."

ANIMATION EVOLVES

Animation has always been cinema's wildest playground. Long before superheroes dominated screens or CGI worlds stretched beyond the horizon, artists were bending reality frame by frame, building entire universes from pencil lines, ink, color, clay, paper, and eventually code. If live-action filmmaking taught audiences how stories could move, animation taught them how stories could fly.

Before people had VHS, streaming, or digital anything, movement started with drawings. Early animators discovered that if they changed an image slightly from frame to frame and played those frames quickly, the world would suddenly breathe. That simple discovery set off a chain reaction of creativity.

Artists like Winsor McCay pushed animation forward with precision. *Gertie the Dinosaur* wasn't just a cartoon character, it was one of the first personalities ever drawn into motion. Every gesture felt intentional, like the creature had a mind of its own. These early works proved animation was a storytelling force.

As studios grew, artists refined techniques that remain the backbone of modern animation. Hand-drawn frames, painted backgrounds, character models, timing charts, storyboards, and the principles of squash and stretch shaped the grammar of animated movement.

Cartoons, Anime, and the Many Branches of Animation

The world began to notice that animation branched out into cultures, styles, beliefs, and artistic instincts. American cartoons grew loud, expressive, comedic, and exaggerated. Characters like Mickey, Bugs Bunny, and Popeye thrived on rhythm, slapstick timing, and bold personality.

Japanese animation took shape with a different heart. Anime focused on emotional stillness, atmosphere, detailed backgrounds, layered storytelling, and characters who carried entire worlds behind their eyes. Even when the action exploded, the quiet moments held just as much weight.

Key differences took shape:

- American cartoons often favored motion and humor.
- Anime leaned into emotion, silence, sharp detail, and cinematic framing.
- Western animation often reset characters each episode.
- Anime usually pushed long arcs, growth, consequences, and world-building.

Neither style replaced the other. They grew side by side, inspiring and borrowing from each other.

The Rise of the Disney Renaissance

In the late 1980s and early 1990s, Disney entered a new era with projects that revived the studio's storytelling force. *The Little Mermaid, Beauty and the Beast, Aladdin,* and *The Lion King* blended music, drama, humor, and character journeys with extraordinary craftsmanship.

Hand-drawn frames flowed with warmth. Characters carried emotional clarity. Songs became narrative engines. Color palettes guided feeling. These films shaped childhoods worldwide and proved that animation could compete with any blockbuster.

While the Disney Renaissance filled screens with spectacle, Studio Ghibli elevated animation through atmosphere and grace. Hayao Miyazaki and Isao Takahata built films that felt like whispered dreams.

Wind brushing through grass, food sizzling gently in a pan, spirits drifting through forests, trains gliding over water. Ghibli stories carried a sense of gentleness even in the face of danger. Films like *Spirited Away*, *Princess Mononoke*, and *My Neighbor Totoro* showed audiences that animation wasn't only for children, and that quiet scenes could be as unforgettable as battles.

Pixar and the Digital Leap

As technology grew, computers entered the art form. Pixar stood at the front of this revolution with *Toy Story*, the first fully computer-animated feature. Digital animation brought new tools:

- lighting that mimicked real physics
- 3D models with depth and texture
- environments that stretched far beyond painted backdrops

Even with new technology, Pixar stayed anchored in emotion. Films like *Up*, *Finding Nemo*, and *Inside Out* proved that the heart of animation wasn't the technique but the truth inside the story.

While digital animation expanded possibilities, stop-motion held onto its tactile charm. Studios like Aardman and Laika built characters from clay, wire, fabric, and foam, adjusting them one frame at a time. Every movement carried texture. Every shadow came from real light.

Films like *Coraline*, *Kubo and the Two Strings*, and *Wallace and Gromit* revealed that handcrafted motion still held magic.

Today's animation mixes everything. Artists blend:

- hand-drawn lines inside 3D worlds
- painted textures over digital bodies
- motion-capture data with animated expression
- anime style with Western color and timing

Films like *Spider-Verse* pushed animation into a new dimension, breaking rules to create a visual rhythm that felt both comic-book inspired and completely fresh.

Animation doesn't depend on the real world. It bends, shapes, stretches, floats, melts, transforms, and reimagines everything we think we know. It invites emotion in unexpected ways and helps audiences travel through futures, myths, memories, and dreams. Anime lovers, cartoon fans, CGI enthusiasts, stop-motion admirers, and hybrid-tech explorers all stand on the same ground: animation moves because imagination moves, and the evolution isn't over. If anything, it is just warming up.

WHEN CINEMA GREW WINGS

The worlds in this chapter weren't built in studios alone. They lived in streets humming with hip-hop, in driveways where kids copied karate moves from Hong Kong tapes, in living rooms glowing with VHS static, in sketchbooks of future animators, in bedrooms where fans collected posters and practiced cosplay before the word became popular.

Movies became rituals, identities, communities, rhythms, memories. Blockbusters turned theaters into temples of spectacle. Superfans turned stories into culture. Hip-hop, horror, and global voices poured lived experience onto the screen. VHS handed the remote to a new generation. Animation turned imagination into something you could feel with your whole chest.

Cinema expanded in every direction at once. This was the era where:

- stories stretched into galaxies and mixtapes
- characters felt bigger than fiction
- fandoms started becoming families
- creators outside the mainstream carved their own lanes
- animation unlocked entire emotional universes

And underneath it all was the same spark: people searching for themselves in the stories they loved.

Now that you've journeyed through the age of spectacle, fandom, rebellion, VHS, and animated evolution, take a moment to look back at your own memories. What movies shaped you? What worlds felt like home? Which characters made you feel seen? Cinema in this era didn't just change the world. It changed people.

To close this chapter, here's a space for you to explore that connection in your own voice.

THE VHS REFLECTION CHALLENGE

Don't worry, this isn't homework or a test; it's simply an invitation or a chance to step into your own cinematic memory.

1. What Does VHS Mean to You?

Before you search for anything, write down what the letters make you think of. A sound? A memory? A texture? A guess? Trust your intuition first.

2. Imagine Holding a VHS for the First Time

Picture the weight of it. The clack of the plastic. The way the tape inside feels like it holds secrets. Describe that moment in your own words.

3. If Your Favorite Movie Was a VHS...

Which scenes would you rewind nonstop? Which line would you memorize? Which moment would get fuzzy from overplaying?

4. Drop Into Your Own Fandom

Bring your world into this. What anime, cartoon, or animated film made you fall in love? What moment from that story felt like it was made just for you?

5. The Cover Art Challenge

Imagine designing a VHS cover for a movie you love. What colors would you choose? What pose? What symbols? How would you tell the world, using only an image, "This story changed me"?

6. Why Movies Matter to You

Write a few lines about what cinema gives you. Comfort? Escape? Courage? New ways of seeing?

This is your space to reflect, laugh, remember, or even dream.

Cinema became a universe in this era. And you, whether you realize it or not, are part of that universe.

CHAPTER 6

WHEN MOVIES SLIPPED INTO THE DIGITAL WORLD

"There is no spoon."
— The Matrix (1999)

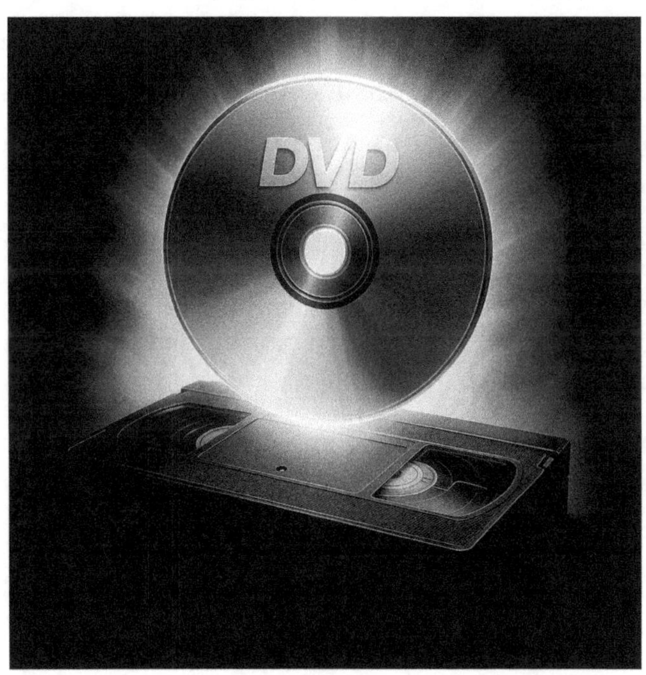

1999 → 2010

Cinema had been shaking cities, filling theaters, and echoing through living rooms, but the turn of the century shifted the pulse again. This time, the magic didn't rise from projectors or VHS tapes. It sparked from glowing monitors in bedrooms, computer labs, internet cafés, and school libraries where kids clicked through pages that loaded one pixel at a time.

Screens didn't just grow brighter; they multiplied. Stories weren't waiting for release dates; they were bouncing through email chains, early forums, fan sites covered in blinking GIFs, and DVD menus packed with secrets. Teens started exploring film through search bars, downloads, burned discs, blog posts, AMVs, and fan theories typed out at two in the morning.

Everything felt wide open. The culture loosened, the world became louder, funnier, faster, and more connected. Someone on one side of the planet could share a clip, and someone on the other side of the ocean could react to it minutes later. Korean dramas spread through friend groups. Anime fansubs circulated like hidden treasure. Trailers lit up group chats. YouTube gave everyday people a stage, and DVDs opened a backstage door to filmmaking tricks nobody had seen before.

Cinema didn't stay put anymore. It stretched, traveled, reshaped itself, and flowed directly into the hands of the audience. This was the moment when fans became creators, creators became communities, and movies found a new home across screens both big and small.

THE DVD ERA

Before the magic hit living rooms, the name itself carried meaning. DVD stood for ***Digital Versatile Disc***, created through a collaboration between companies like Toshiba, Panasonic, and Sony during the mid-1990s. It arrived as the successor to VHS, using lasers instead of magnetic tape to read information. That shift alone opened the door to higher picture quality, cleaner audio, and the ability to pack far more data into a single disc.

Once upon a time, there was a silver disc that felt almost futuristic the first time it hit a player. that felt almost futuristic the first time it hit a player. DVDs arrived with a quiet confidence, slipping into homes and instantly changing how people watched, studied, collected, and obsessed over movies. This was a whole new experience.

A VHS tape felt warm, nostalgic, and familiar, but the moment a DVD loaded, everything changed. The picture sharpened. Colors popped. Sound wrapped around the room with clarity that felt unreal. You didn't have to rewind anything; you simply pressed a button, and the story jumped wherever you wanted.

DVDs carried a clean, crisp elegance that caught everyone off guard. They felt modern, compact, and efficient. You could slip three or four into a backpack and bring them to a friend's house without feeling like you were hauling bricks.

DVD menus turned movies into playgrounds. Animations danced across the screen, and music loops pulled you into a film's mood before it even started. Backgrounds changed with each selection. For teens discovering DVDs in the early 2000s, menu screens felt like opening a digital portal.

Then came the special features: Behind-the-scenes footage, deleted scenes, bloopers, director commentaries, storyboard comparisons, concept art galleries, mini-documentaries explaining how effects were created, tutorials where animators shared sketches or studios revealed the tricks behind stunts, and many more features. For kids who dreamed of filmmaking, these bonus features felt like gold because DVDs didn't just show movies; they taught how movies worked.

The Collector Era

DVDs became more than discs; they established identity. People lined shelves with cases arranged by color, genre, director, or pure chaotic instinct. Some teens built entire collections of anime box sets. Others hunted for limited editions with metallic covers, holographic slips, or bonus discs tucked inside.

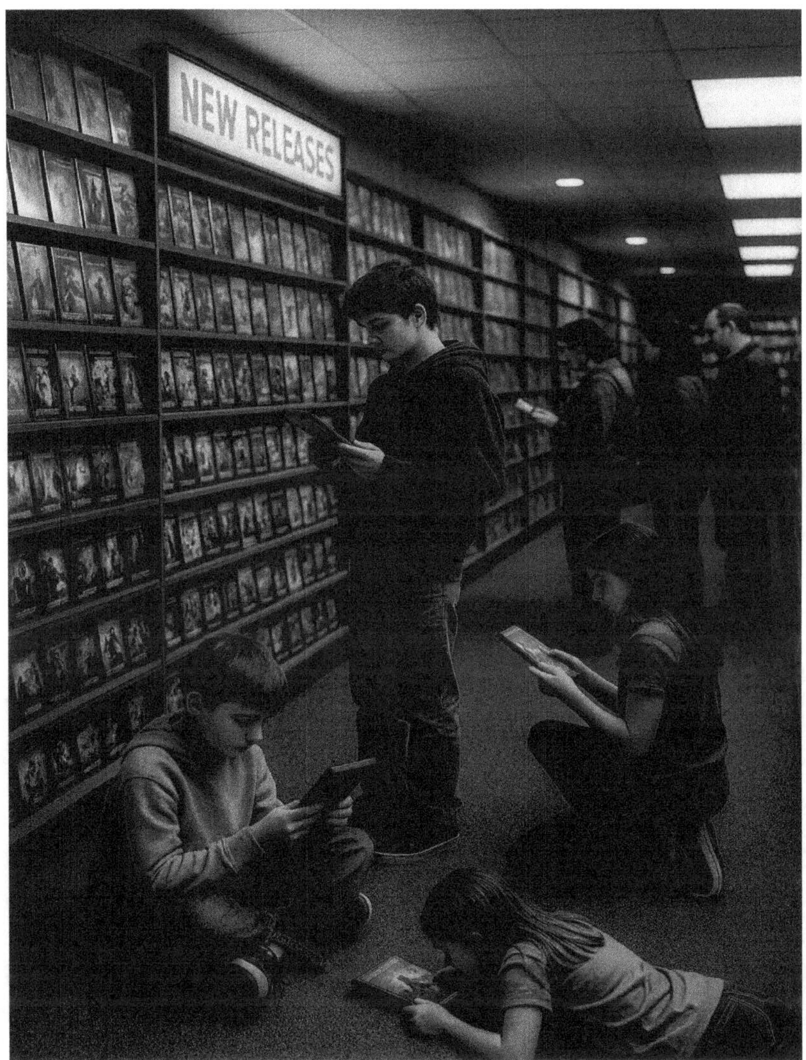

Saturday trips to DVD stores became events. Browsing aisles felt like exploring a gallery; every case had personality, and every cover told a story.

DVD culture encouraged:

- lending movies to friends
- discovering hidden gems

- rewatching favorites with commentary
- bonding over collections
- exploring international cinema through imports

The disc became a passport to worlds you chose, not schedules forced on you.

As the web expanded, DVDs formed a bridge between physical and digital culture.

People joined forums to share recommendations. Fans wrote long reviews that combined emotion with analysis. Others ripped scenes to make AMVs, edits, or meme clips. Teens passed around burned discs like mixtapes, trading titles, genres, and entire vibes.

DVDs carried movies into the digital era one disc at a time, giving fans new ways to watch, study, share, and connect through stories. Ultimately, they influenced an entire generation of film lovers.

THE INTERNET ARRIVES

The moment the internet flickered into everyday life, movies found a new home, a new audience, and a completely new rhythm. Stories didn't wait for theaters, TV schedules, or DVD releases anymore. They traveled through dial-up tones, glowing screens, early chat rooms, and tabs that loaded slowly but felt like portals. Teens discovered films not only through advertisements, but also through message boards, fan sites, shared links, and whispers between friends.

Before social media became a second language, movie fans gathered in places that felt like secret meeting grounds. Forums, fan blogs, Geocities pages, and message boards became tiny digital cities dedicated to the movies people loved.

Someone in Chicago could debate plot twists with someone in Seoul. Teens swapped theories, posted fan art, shared soundtrack playlists, and recommended films across continents. Conversations lasted hours, sometimes days, and every reply felt like opening a door to someone else's imagination.

These spaces were chaotic, colorful, messy, and full of inside jokes. But that chaos felt alive.

Fansubs, AMVs, and the Rise of Global Anime Culture

Anime didn't spread because studios pushed it. It spread because fans did. Fansubbing groups translated episodes, added subtitles, compressed files, and shared them across the internet long before streaming platforms caught on. These groups introduced entire generations to series that would have stayed hidden behind borders.

Meanwhile, AMVs *(Anime Music Videos)* became the emotional backbone of early online fandom. Teens blended clips from *Naruto, Bleach, Inuyasha, Sailor Moon, Fullmetal Alchemist,* and *Dragon Ball Z* with music that defined their era. Soft rock, hyperstylized edits, dramatic transitions, and emotional storytelling all mixed into something powerful. AMVs turned editing into a global language.

Movies found new life online through:

- character shrines
- episode breakdowns
- fanfic communities

- pixel art avatars
- homemade wallpapers
- early meme formats

People built entire websites dedicated to a single film, a character, or even a single scene. Reviews appeared on personal blogs where emotion mattered more than technical critique. Screenshots became jokes, and quotes turned into catchphrases. I mean, who doesn't know of Madhara Uchiha's Pain speech???

Cinema suddenly felt shareable.

The First Viral Moments

Clips from movies and shows traveled between inboxes like treasure. Reaction videos appeared in tiny windows whilst trailers leaked early and spread faster than studios could react. The internet cracked open the distribution wall and let audiences pass stories around freely, and through all of this, something important happened: Fans discovered their voices.

They didn't just enjoy films, they shaped the energy around them and carried stories to new countries, uplifted hidden gems, gave international films new lands to grow in, and built communities where no official platform existed. Cinema entered the digital world, and the digital world answered with curiosity, creativity, and a loud, unstoppable culture of its own.

THE RISE OF YOUTUBE

The internet was already buzzing with fan sites and message boards, but then a new idea stepped into the room; three former PayPal employees, **Steve Chen**, **Chad Hurley**, and **Jawed Karim**, sitting on a simple problem: *Why is it so hard to share a video online?* File sizes were messy. Formats kept breaking. Emails couldn't handle large files. Watching or sending a clip felt like trying to push a sofa through a mailbox.

Their solution started as a joke, then grew into a spark, and eventually became a revolution.

They called it **YouTube**; a name that blended two truths: *You*, the individual creator, and *Tube*, the old slang for television. A personal TV for the whole world, and a place where the screen belonged to everyone.

The first video uploaded, *Me at the Zoo*, by Karim, felt ordinary on the surface, but it carried a quiet promise: *anyone can do this.* That energy changed everything.

A New Stage Opens

As soon as the site went live, something wild happened. Teens, creators, film lovers, anime fans, comedians, gamers, dancers, reviewers, musicians, everyone stepped forward. Bedrooms became studios, school halls turned into film sets, and backyards hosted lightsaber duels.

There was no algorithm ruling the world yet, no polished brands, no professional lighting like nowadays, just pure expression and creativity.

Eventually, movie trailers escaped theaters and TV schedules. A studio could drop a teaser at midnight, and by breakfast, entire continents were watching. Fans paused, zoomed in, caught details, swapped theories, and created edits before anyone slept. A single trailer release felt like a global heartbeat.

Later on, fans turned YouTube into a creative playground. Scenes from *Shrek, Twilight, Avatar: The Last Airbender, Naruto,* and every fandom imaginable were sliced, remixed, re-scored, exaggerated, flipped, slowed, sped up, and turned into art or comedy.

AMVs and the Rise of Online Emotion

If the early internet gave anime a voice, YouTube gave it a stage.

AMVs grew sharper, edits became a form of storytelling, power-ups synced with bass drops, heartbreak scenes matched soft vocals, and fight montages glowed with dramatic timing.

For anime fans, YouTube felt like home, a place where they were understood.

Reactors, Reviewers, and Film Criticism 2.0

People didn't need film school to have an opinion. They set up cameras, spoke with honesty, and built communities around:

- reactions
- breakdowns
- symbolism analysis
- animation dissections
- genre deep dives

Viewers learned more about cinematic craft from YouTubers with passion than from entire academic textbooks. Furthermore, creators crafted horror shorts with nothing but hallway lights and timing. Comedy skits exploded from small bedrooms. Animators uploaded progress tests. Indie directors filmed chase scenes with borrowed cameras. YouTube became more like a film studio that didn't need permission. It also birthed a generation of creators who didn't wait to be discovered. They built their own platforms, audiences, and their own style. Fame no longer traveled from Hollywood downward. It grew from ordinary rooms upward.

YouTube expanded cinema, turning millions of viewers into creators and giving film culture a pulse that beat across the world.

WORLD CINEMA GOES GLOBAL

YouTube didn't just change how people watched videos, it changed how people watched *the world*. One moment you were catching a movie trailer at home, the next you were streaming a concert in another country, joining a Bible study online, attending a class across the world, or watching someone cook a meal you had never heard of. Distance melted, borders softened, and culture moved at the speed of a click.

Movies felt that shift immediately.

A film didn't need a Hollywood release anymore to find an audience. It needed curiosity, a link, a recommendation, a clip that echoed across timelines, or a moment that spoke to someone far away. Stories that once stayed local began traveling, one upload at a time. This is when global cinema stepped forward with confidence.

The Korean Wave

Korean creators arrived with stories built from honesty, humor, heartbreak, and ambition. K-dramas spread through friend groups like a secret treasure. One person watched an episode, told a cousin, the cousin told a classmate, and suddenly the whole school was hooked. These dramas carried:

- layered relationships
- emotional pacing
- stylish cinematography
- characters who felt familiar, flawed, and real

Then came Korean films that hit worldwide screens with force. *Oldboy*, *Train to Busan (One of my favorites)*, *The Host*, and many others proved that Korean storytelling blended emotion, spectacle, and creativity in ways that felt refreshing. K-cinema literally earned it.

Nollywood

Across Africa, storytellers in Nigeria were building an entire film industry from pure determination. Nollywood grew from street markets, handheld cameras, and stories rooted in community. Films were produced quickly, shared widely, and loved deeply. People gathered around TVs to watch tales of:

- family
- tradition
- faith
- rivalry
- love
- humor

Nollywood carried its own rhythm. The pacing felt different, the acting felt direct, and even the emotion felt close to home. Before long, it became one of the largest film industries in the world.

Latin America

Meanwhile, directors across Mexico, Brazil, Argentina, and beyond were crafting some of the most powerful films of the era. Their stories carried political tension, magical realism, social commentary, and visually stunning craftsmanship. Filmmakers like Alfonso Cuarón, Alejandro G. Iñárritu, and Guillermo del Toro stepped onto the world stage with films that blended fantasy, reality, and deep emotion. Latin American cinema carried soul.

Asia's Continued Rise

Hong Kong's action choreography, Japanese horror, and Southeast Asian storytelling all found new audiences through digital sharing. Clips from martial arts scenes, emotional moments, or beautifully animated sequences spread across the internet like sparks. Fans didn't need official releases. They found content through:

- recommendations
- uploads
- subtitles created by communities

The world opened itself to new rhythms, new faces, and new languages.

For the first time, film culture felt like a conversation instead of a hierarchy. Stories crossed oceans faster than studios could track. Teens grew up watching content from five continents without even realizing it. Cinema didn't just belong to one country anymore. It belonged to every screen it could reach.

EARLY CGI & DIGITAL FILMMAKING

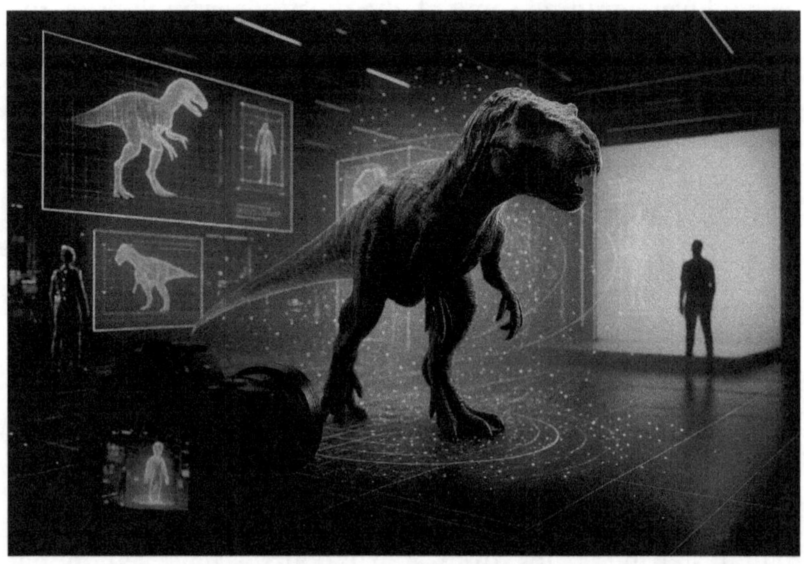

Global cinema had already begun moving at the speed of the internet. Trailers went viral, clips spread across borders, and films we talked about, like *Train to Busan*, *Star Wars*, and *The Host*, traveled across screens with a force that felt electric. Audiences could feel something shifting. Stories were getting bigger, faster, stranger, and more ambitious. The reason sat quietly beneath the spectacle: a brand-new toolbox: CGI.

Computer-generated imagery stepped into filmmaking like a new instrument added to an orchestra. Not replacing the old tools, but expanding the sound. Suddenly, filmmakers didn't have to ask, "Can this be done?" They asked, "How far can we go?"

Digital effects started small, almost experimental. Filmmakers tested wireframes, simple shapes, digital textures, and early models that looked nothing like the realism we know today.

The major turning point arrived with *Jurassic Park*. Audiences watched massive dinosaurs move with muscle, breath, and weight. What looked impossible just a few years earlier became a cinematic roar.

The New Tools Behind the Curtain

Digital filmmaking unlocked:

- virtual creatures
- expansive environments
- motion capture performances
- digital stunts
- seamless green screen worlds

Actors performed in empty rooms while effects teams added galaxies, storms, cities, and monsters. Directors could build entire landscapes from imagination. Motion capture pushed this further. Performers acted out movements while wearing suits covered in tiny markers, and computers translated every gesture into digital characters. Emotion became data, and data became art.

Film Styles Shift

Movies began to stretch in new directions; action sequences moved faster, worlds grew larger, magic felt more detailed, and Sci-fi leaned deeper into the surreal.

Stories like:

- *Star Wars: The Phantom Menace*
- *The Matrix*
- *Spider-Man*
- *The Lord of the Rings*

All these used CGI to expand storytelling beyond physical limits. Cameras swooped through digital skies. Characters leapt across impossible distances. Battles unfolded across landscapes too large to build.

CGI also changed animation forever. Studios like Pixar proved that fully digital movies could carry emotion, heart, and cinematic weight. The same principles guiding practical effects: lighting, texture, timing, were now applied through software. Animation and digital film began growing together.

Even with digital tools rising, filmmakers blended practical effects with CGI to maintain realism. Miniatures, props, puppets, and physical sets still grounded many scenes. The balance between digital and practical work shaped some of the most iconic films of the early 2000s.

With CGI available, imagination expanded, and every genre opened new doors:

- horror crafted digital nightmares
- action leapt beyond gravity
- fantasy embraced entire realms

- sci-fi explored futures with depth

Filmmakers stepped into a playground where ideas no longer feared limitation.

FRANCHISES & SHARED UNIVERSES

By the time CGI opened new doors and global cinema found fresh momentum, something else began brewing in the background. Fans weren't just watching films anymore; they were following characters, waiting for sequels, memorizing lore, quoting spells, choosing houses, joining clans, debating timelines, and carrying entire worlds in their heads. Stories no longer closed their doors at the credits.

They expanded.

They connected.

They built universes.

The Era of the Epic — Harry Potter Casts Its Spell

When the first *Harry Potter* film hit screens, it felt like a global ceremony. Families lined up in wizard robes, and teens tried out accents, while adults proudly joined them. Every ticket felt like a train ride straight to Hogwarts. Magic moved through the air literally and emotionally. Spells flew like poetry:

- "Wingardium Leviosa" for lifting spirits (and feathers)
- "Expecto Patronum" for chasing away darkness
- "Lumos" for lighting up more than rooms
- "Accio" for calling things closer, including childhood wonder

Fans didn't leave the story behind when the credits rolled; they lived in it. They asked themselves which house fit their soul, drew fan art of creatures, and debated characters like they were classmates. Harry Potter developed into more than just a franchise; it became a culture.

Middle-earth Rises — The Ring, the Quest, the Whisper of "My Precious"

Then came a journey carved from myth, mountains, friendship, and one whisper that echoed across an entire generation.

The Lord of the Rings was quite an experience. Every frame felt handcrafted, and every landscape carried history. Every sword swing felt like it had weight, and even the characters were just on point: Frodo, Sam, Legolas, Aragorn, Gollum (I mean, who'd hate him?), they all stepped out of the screen with personalities that felt ancient and human at once. The moment Gollum rasped, "my precious," the world gained a new phrase that slipped into jokes, memes, and everyday conversations. Till date, Gollum still has that fresh, catchy vibe.

Trilogies became a new art form. Fans returned year after year, growing with the characters. Middle-earth felt like a second home.

From the Streets to the Stars — Fast & Furious Builds a Family

While wizards and warriors shaped fantasy worlds, another universe was roaring to life on asphalt: Fast cars, family, loyalty, outrageous missions, and unbreakable bonds. The *Fast*

& Furious franchise built a universe that felt grounded in heart and carried by adrenaline. Teens quoted lines, downloaded soundtracks, and argued about which character they related to the most. The streets became their own myth.

Superheroes Find Their Blueprint — Marvel's Quiet Beginning

Before the MCU exploded into billions of dollars and a universe spanning galaxies, it started with a simple idea: stories don't have to stand alone.

Early hints appeared: Post-credit scenes, character crossovers, references hiding in dialog, and heroes who lived in the same world even if they hadn't met yet. Fans caught the signals, and universe-building became the new heartbeat of cinema.

These stories invited audiences to grow with a world they were creating beyond just one film. Fans learned to:

- track lore across years
- follow character arcs like personal journeys
- celebrate inside jokes and subtle references
- predict connections before they happened
- feel belonging inside fictional worlds

Shared universes gave people something rare: the feeling that their imagination mattered. For millions, these franchises created a community. They were worlds where every fan could choose their place: wizard, ranger, hobbit, Avenger, gearhead, or hero of their own making.

WHEN CINEMA STEPPED INTO THE FUTURE

The digital age didn't arrive with a whisper. It came through glowing screens, loading bars, dial-up tones, shared links, bookmarked fan pages, and communities that gathered long before social media had a name. Movies no longer lived in theaters or on shelves alone; they lived in conversations, edits, forums, comment sections, and timelines. They became part of daily life.

Furthermore. Stories didn't wait for release dates. They moved through inboxes, YouTube queues, fan edits, online reactions, AMVs, and global recommendations that traveled faster than studios could predict. One moment you were watching a trailer, the next moment you were deep in a discussion with someone halfway across the planet. Cinema stretched across borders not because corporations pushed it, but because fans carried it.

This chapter captured a turning point when art stopped being a one-way broadcast and became a shared experience. People didn't just watch movies anymore; they shaped the culture around them. They built communities, became creators, and ultimately, they made the digital world a second home for storytelling.

Key Takeaways

- DVDs gave fans backstage access to filmmaking and turned viewers into students of cinema.
- The internet connected film lovers across continents, forming communities before social media existed.

- YouTube handed everyday people the tools to create, remix, critique, and build their own audiences.
- Global cinema rose through passion and curiosity, not gatekeepers.
- CGI expanded the canvas, giving imagination more room to breathe.
- Franchises created universes where fans felt like they belonged.

The world didn't just watch movies anymore, it participated in them. I mean, think of a few years back when you waited for the release of the Black Panther. So here's a digital explorer challenge for you to play with:

Pick one or pick three. Follow your interest.

1. Search for the most-viewed YouTube video of all time.

Compare it to the most-viewed movie trailer ever uploaded. What does that say about what people watch today?

2. Watch an AMV.

Choose one at random. Study the editing, feel the emotion, and notice how anime and music blend into something entirely new.

3. Explore a film industry outside your own.

Search for a trailer from:

- Korea
- Nigeria (Nollywood)
- Japan

- Mexico
- India

Find one movie you've never heard of before today. Let curiosity guide you.

4. Revisit the first YouTube video ever uploaded.

Me at the Zoo is only a few seconds long. Think about how that tiny clip sparked a platform that changed cinema forever.

5. Look up the top-grossing film franchise today.

Watch the trailer for its first movie and its latest movie. Notice how visuals, tone, effects, and pacing evolved.

CHAPTER 7:

THE FUTURE ARRIVES

"Wakanda forever."
— Black Panther (2018)

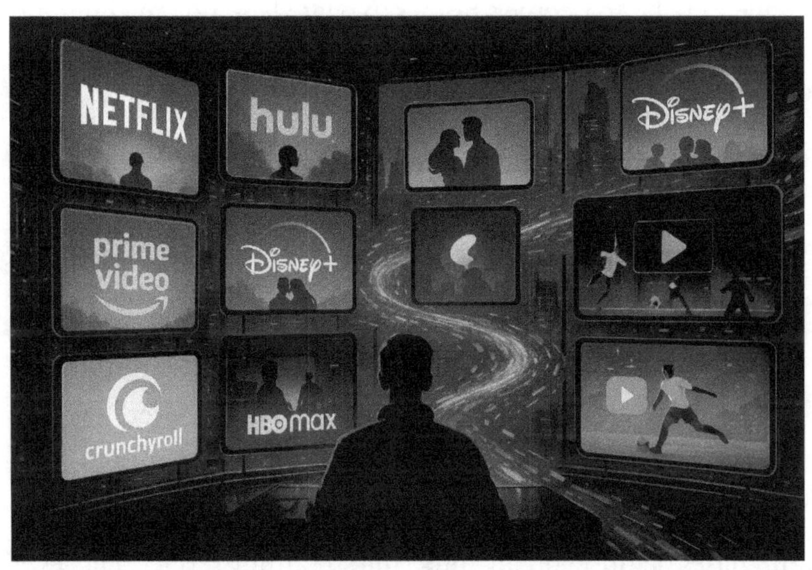

2010 → Now

Long before Netflix became a household name and long before endless scrolling became a nightly ritual, the ground for streaming was already forming in the digital world. The internet grew stronger, devices grew smaller, and people began consuming stories faster and more flexibly. YouTube proved that videos could travel through screens instantly. Fans shared clips, creators uploaded freely, and audiences discovered content at their own pace.

That momentum raised a question for tech innovators: *What if movies and shows moved the same way?*

In the late 1990s, Reed Hastings and Marc Randolph explored this idea while building a company that originally mailed DVDs to people's homes. No late fees, no long lines, no hunting for the last copy of a new release. A simple delivery system sparked interest, but streaming was the real dream waiting in the background. When technology improved, that dream opened its eyes.

Netflix took its first step online with a library that streamed directly through the web. The shift felt subtle at first, almost experimental, but the idea carried power.

Other platforms watched closely. Hulu focused on TV shows and partnered with major networks. Prime Video grew from Amazon's massive ecosystem, offering rentals and purchases before evolving into a full streaming service. Disney+ gathered its iconic worlds under one roof. Crunchyroll built a space where anime fans could gather without borders.

However, streaming didn't appear suddenly; it rose layer by layer, shaped by:

- Advances in internet speed
- The success of YouTube's sharing culture
- The rise of personal devices
- global interest in on-demand entertainment
- a generation that valued choice and convenience

Once these pieces fit together, the world stepped into a new rhythm. People created watch lists as long as novels. Entire seasons appeared in a single drop, group chats filled with reactions, trailers spread within minutes, and students streamed episodes between classes. Families built rituals around premieres, and communities formed around shows written in languages they had never spoken before. Essentially, streaming expanded how stories reached people.

The experience became flexible, personal, global, and fast. Stories no longer waited for schedules or physical formats. They traveled freely, flowing through screens and into everyday life with ease.

This new era reshaped how films, series, and animated worlds connected with audiences, opening the door for everything that comes next.

VIRTUAL PRODUCTION

Before streaming taking over living rooms and phones, filmmakers around the world were wrestling with a new question: '*How do we shoot scenes that feel bigger than anything we can build, without losing the natural magic of real performances?*'

Green screens worked, but something felt missing. Actors stared at blank walls. Directors imagined worlds that the crew couldn't see. Scenes needed emotion, presence, and texture. Everyone wanted something that blended imagination with reality. The search for a better tool pushed filmmakers toward an idea that once sounded impossible: creating full environments in real time.

At this point, video games had already mastered the art of building digital worlds that moved smoothly and reacted instantly. Filmmakers had noticed this. If a game engine could create a sunset or a desert or a fantasy planet on the fly, why not blend that power with live-action film?

Unreal Engine stepped into the spotlight. Artists began testing real-time environments that shifted with camera movement. Digital mountains rose, planets glowed, cities expanded in seconds, and for the first time, entire landscapes lived inside a screen, ready to respond the moment a camera moved. The dream of virtual production had a pulse.

Then everything changed when a new kind of soundstage appeared. Instead of green walls, filmmakers surrounded actors with massive LED panels that displayed living, breathing digital worlds. They called it *'the Volume.'*

When the camera tilted, the world inside the LED walls shifted naturally, matching the perspective. It's more like sunlight moved, shadows adjusted, and reflections landed perfectly on armor, glass, metal, and skin. Actors weren't pretending anymore; they stood inside the worlds they were exploring. Directors pointed to mountains that existed only digitally, but felt real in the room. Crews watched scenes unfold inside places that would have been impossible to build by hand. The Volume turned imagination into something you could walk through (Kane, 2025).

This approach offered more than visual beauty. It offered:

- natural lighting that matched the digital world
- complete control over weather, time of day, and atmosphere
- the ability to shoot fantasy scenes without expensive travel
- real environments for actors to react to
- fewer limitations on creativity

The result felt grounded and cinematic, even when the story stretched across galaxies. Eventually, directors blended real props with digital landscapes. Cinematographers painted scenes with light that wrapped naturally around characters, and VFX artists worked hand in hand with camera operators. The process became fluid, collaborative, and faster.

In today's world, real-time environments continue to evolve. Independent filmmakers experiment with smaller versions of the Volume. Game developers collaborate with movie studios, and digital artists build worlds that react to every movement.

ARTIFICIAL INTELLIGENCE

2015 → Now

Virtual production opened the door to digital worlds that blended with physical sets, and that momentum naturally pushed filmmakers toward something even more transformative. This shift stepped into everyday life through phones, laptops, and apps anyone could explore.

Artificial intelligence made the leap from quiet background software to a public breakthrough. One moment, AI existed in research labs, the next, entire communities were generating artwork, drafting ideas, experimenting with voices, crafting scenes, and editing videos with tools that felt almost magical. Teens used AI to remix songs. Animators tested concepts in minutes. Writers shaped characters through interactive prompts. Everyday creators found shortcuts that once belonged only to massive studios.

Content creators cleaned audio for podcasts, shaped visual concepts for storyboards, designed characters, experimented with motion styles, and refined scripts through tools that suggested rhythm and structure. These same tools stepped into professional production pipelines with surprising harmony.

Editors used AI to arrange timelines for smoother workflows, and sound teams lifted dialog from chaotic recordings with impressive clarity. Animators built early movement tests without long rendering waits. Colorists explored moods by instantly shifting palettes. Directors visualized scenes in seconds rather than hours.

Filmmaking gained new momentum as de-aging techniques reached subtle realism, and performance scanning recorded micro-expressions once missed by traditional tech. AI touched set design by generating mood boards and concepts that sparked imagination. VFX teams crafted backgrounds with layers of detail built from both human skill and digital assistance.

Even audiences indirectly shaped AI's rise. Viral filters, face-swap trends, remixed scenes, and fan edits created a culture where digital manipulation felt familiar and creative. This wave inspired filmmakers to explore narratives centered on AI itself. Stories like *Her*, *Ex Machina*, *M3GAN*, and *The Creator* hit screens with themes that mirrored the world's growing relationship with intelligent tools.

AI expanded what artists could attempt without replacing the heart behind their work. It lifted the heavy tasks, accelerated the technical steps, and left more room for vision, emotion, and the human instinct that storytelling depends on.

The next evolution of cinema is not a machine telling stories. It is a machine helping storytellers dream bigger.

DIGITAL DOUBLES, SYNTHETIC STARS, AND THE NEW FACE OF PERFORMANCE

While AI entered creative spaces as a quiet assistant, one development rose quickly into the spotlight: the ability to recreate a face, a voice, or an entire performance with astonishing precision. Deepfake technology and digital doubles came into the acting industry filled with potential, curiosity, and questions, the industry continues to explore (Barney et al., 2025)

Long before the term "deepfake" became popular, filmmakers experimented with digital likeness. Visual effects teams studied muscle movement, skin texture, light behavior, and aging patterns. Early attempts appeared in fantasy and science fiction, where digital characters emerged from performance capture suits.

Audiences witnessed the breakthrough through figures like Gollum in *The Lord of the Rings*. Andy Serkis delivered a full emotional performance while artists translated every gesture into a digital creature. That collaboration revealed a truth: technology could enhance acting rather than replace it.

Deepfake tools grew from machine-learning research. These systems learned patterns through thousands of images and built models capable of recreating faces with remarkable accuracy.

Suddenly, creators on social platforms experimented with:

- face swaps
- voice replication
- re-imagined scenes
- restored footage

A single laptop handled work that once required entire studios. What once felt like science fiction turned into everyday creativity.

Studios began exploring digital doubles for storytelling needs. Examples include scenes where actors portrayed younger versions of themselves, moments requiring continuity after schedule changes, and performances shaped from reference scans.

One notable case involved recreating Peter Cushing's likeness for *Rogue One*, crafted through careful scanning, voice study, and performance reference by another actor. The goal aimed to maintain story integrity while honoring a legacy. Another example appeared when filmmakers shaped younger versions of characters in *Tron: Legacy* and later in several superhero films.

These processes demanded precision. Actors collaborated with digital teams, delivering expressions and movements while technology extended those performances into new forms.

Archives around the world began using advanced facial and motion analysis tools to restore old scenes with greater clarity. Classic performances with damaged frames gained new sharpness. Sound improvements elevated emotional impact. Families and historians gained access to footage once considered unusable.

A vivid example surfaced when a short sequence from an early twentieth-century film was enhanced through neural tools, revealing facial details unseen for more than one hundred years. Viewers described the experience as "meeting someone from the past." Moments like this highlighted how technology could strengthen connections rather than reduce authenticity.

Identity, Consent, and Ownership

As with every powerful tool, deepfake technology introduced questions. Creators, actors, unions, and studios entered discussions about:

- personal likeness rights
- permission for digital recreation
- ethical storytelling
- long-term use of synthetic performers

Several production companies now require clear agreements before any digital scan takes place. Performers receive protection around how and when their likeness may appear.

Digital doubles offer opportunities rather than threats when used responsibly. Stunt sequences gain safety through digital assistance. Fantasy worlds gain expressive creatures shaped from human emotion. Historical films recreate environments that no longer exist. Directors shape dreamlike transitions between live-action and digital imagery.

Examples from modern cinema reveal this balance. *Avatar* paired performance capture with digital artistry to shape characters with emotional depth. *Gemini Man* introduced a younger digital counterpart to the lead actor, crafted through months of reference work. Essentially, actors remain central while technology responds to them.

Synthetic stars and digital doubles may continue to evolve, yet the soul of performance still comes from human intention. Technology supports expression, sharpens detail, and expands possibilities.

The next era of storytelling may blend real and digital faces with seamless harmony, offering scenes that feel vivid, imaginative, and emotionally grounded. Digital tools may shape the surface, but human stories shape the heart.

GAMING AND CINEMA

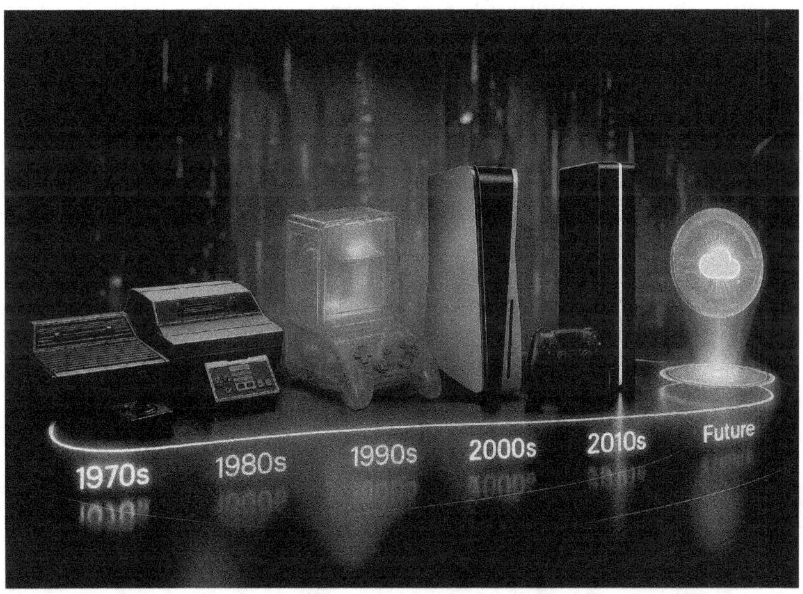

The rise of digital faces and synthetic performances set the stage for something even larger. Once filmmakers saw how technology could reshape characters, their attention shifted toward the one art form that had already mastered digital worlds: gaming.

Games carried a rhythm that felt familiar to cinema. They told stories with emotion, crafted tension, framed action with purpose, and invited audiences into universes built with detail and intention. The difference came from control. Instead of watching a journey unfold, players stepped inside it. This energy pulled film and gaming toward each other until the line between them faded.

Cinematic Games

Long before gaming reached modern scale, certain titles revealed how powerful interactive storytelling could be. Scenes unfolded with pacing, framing, and atmosphere that echoed cinema. Players followed characters through arcs shaped by struggle, growth, and consequence.

Titles like *Metal Gear Solid*, *Final Fantasy X*, *Mass Effect*, *God of War*, and *Uncharted* delivered narratives that blended gameplay with emotional weight. Cutscenes carried the depth of film sequences. Character expressions held nuance, music guided tension, and entire worlds felt alive. Essentially, gamers didn't simply watch these stories; they carried them.

Motion Capture

As games grew more ambitious, developers needed performances that carried soul. Motion capture became a bridge between live-action craft and digital storytelling.

Actors stepped onto stages covered with tracking markers and delivered scenes with full intention. Directors shaped blocking and emotion the same way they would on a film set. Artists translated each expression, gesture, and breath into digital form.

Examples emerged across the industry:

- *The Last of Us* featured performances that shaped a global phenomenon.
- *God of War* presented a father-son story anchored by emotional depth.
- *Detroit: Become Human* explored choice and consequence through expressive characters.

Gamers felt the weight of these performances because the emotion came from real people.

While games borrowed cinematic techniques, cinema borrowed game engines. Real-time rendering allowed directors to walk through digital environments as if they were physical sets. Cameras moved through worlds with the same freedom players experienced.

Unreal Engine became a favorite across studios. Independent filmmakers explored Unity for stylized visuals. Every tool offered speed, flexibility, and creative freedom. This shift helped stories reach new heights. Landscapes changed instantly, lighting reacted naturally, and sets expanded without construction costs. Eventually, filmmakers gained access to worlds limited only by imagination.

Furthermore, gaming introduced something cinema never offered: agency. Choice created a sense of ownership. When players shaped outcomes or guided characters through difficult paths, the emotional impact grew deeper.

Telltale's *The Walking Dead* captured hearts by blending narrative tension with personal decisions. *Life Is Strange* used player choice to heighten vulnerability and empathy. *Detroit:*

Become Human presented branching paths that felt cinematic yet personal. The medium evolved into more than entertainment. It became an expression.

Streaming Culture and Esports Influence Film

Gaming communities expanded through livestreams and reactions. Twitch and YouTube created spaces where millions watched gameplay the same way previous generations watched television.

This culture shaped cinema subtly. Faster pacing, sharper transitions, and emotional beats, guided by collective reactions, have become prevalent in modern productions. Films based on games explored new identities. Titles like *Detective Pikachu*, *Sonic the Hedgehog*, and *The Last of Us* adapted familiar worlds into cinematic experiences with broad appeal.

Games released animations and trailers with the impact of film premieres. Fortnite concerts reached global audiences simultaneously. League of Legends produced shorts that rivaled studio films in style and emotion. Apex Legends and Overwatch expanded lore through beautifully crafted cinematics. These moments proved that modern storytelling stretched far beyond familiar formats.

Cinema and gaming no longer travel on separate paths; they move together. Future stories may unfold through hybrid experiences, immersive environments, interactive choices, and real-time collaboration between player and creator. AI-driven characters may respond with personality, whilst digital worlds grow alongside the audience.

Together, gaming and cinema shaped a future where imagination becomes a space you step into rather than a place you watch.

GLOBAL CREATORS RISE

As technology opened new doors, something powerful started happening outside the major studios. The tools that once belonged only to giant companies now lived on laptops, home desktops, shared school computers, internet cafés, and small production hubs scattered across cities and townships. Creativity began spreading in every direction, shaped by places with their own rhythm, humor, history, and heartbeat. The future of cinema no longer sat in one country; it sat everywhere. For instance:

In South Africa, creators embraced digital tools with sharp instinct. Music videos, short films, VFX experiments, TikTok skits, and indie projects found life through communities that supported one another. Filmmakers blended local languages with global ideas. Visual artists carved new aesthetics through bold lighting, expressive color, and confident storytelling.

Projects like *District 9* proved that South African filmmaking carried grit, texture, and emotional weight. The film's combination of documentary style, sci-fi ambition, and social commentary caught global attention. Success stories like this inspired a new generation to push even further with digital design, animation, and world-building.

Young creators experimented with:

- drone shots
- VFX plug-ins
- animated shorts
- community-driven productions
- online collaborations

Every step proved that great ideas didn't need Hollywood budgets to land with force.

Nollywood had already built one of the largest film industries in the world through speed, creativity, and raw storytelling. As digital tools improved, Nigerian creators embraced visual effects, color grading, and high-quality cinematography with momentum.

Studios in Lagos developed stronger pipelines. VFX teams built creatures, crowds, and action moments with software that once felt out of reach. Directors blended local traditions with modern genres, shaping films that resonated across Africa and the diaspora. Nollywood's strength came from instinct: communities hungry for stories and creators determined to deliver them.

Indian cinema always embraced grand scale, but digital advancements amplified it. Productions across Hyderabad, Mumbai, and Chennai developed massive worlds through CGI that matched emotional storytelling with spectacle.

Films like *Baahubali* and *RRR* showcased bold choreography, dramatic visuals, and seamless blending of practical and digital effects. These films proved that global audiences crave energy and emotion just as much as realism. Animation studios expanded too, shaping characters and environments for both local and international markets. The combination of tradition, cultural myth, and technology created a style that stood proudly on its own.

Korean creators rose with a style that blended precision with emotional punch. The world celebrated dramas and films long before streaming giants caught on, but digital tools gave them even more reach. Korean sci-fi, thrillers, action pieces, and horror titles carried sharp pacing, clean visual storytelling, and fearless imagination. Creators shaped sequences with meticulous framing, layered sound design, and expressive visual effects.

This momentum helped global audiences discover Korean cinema through streaming and social sharing, creating a global wave that grew year after year.

Across Mexico, Brazil, Argentina, and Chile, storytellers built films that moved with poetic energy. Fantasy blended with folklore. Soft magical realism met digital world-building. Directors combined handcrafted creativity with modern tools, shaping experiences that felt both intimate and epic.

International recognition for filmmakers like Guillermo del Toro opened doors for newer creators exploring animation, green screen work, and hybrid formats.

Affordable Tools Changed Everything

The rise of global creators came from access. Knowledge moved freely through online tutorials that guided beginners with clarity and confidence. Editing apps offered tools once reserved for professional studios. Animation platforms gave artists instant ways to share their work. Phone cameras captured cinematic moments with surprising quality. Game engines provided filmmakers with entire worlds to shape and explore.

A teenager with a laptop could build a visual world in a bedroom, whilst a small team in a local studio could create a fantasy realm with passion and smart workflow. A creator on the other side of the world could upload a short film and find an audience overnight.

Cinema spread faster, wider, and deeper than ever. Storytelling no longer depended on geography, and creativity no longer required permission. The world opened its stage, then every creator with vision gained space to shine, and every audience gained access to stories shaped by cultures they had never reached.

This is the era where film became truly global, carried by voices rising from every corner of the world.

THE FUTURE IN YOUR HANDS

Innovation shaped every corner of this chapter, but the heart of it stayed simple: creativity spreads wherever curiosity lives. From digital faces to game engines, from global storytellers to tools that fit inside pockets, the future grew wider because more people stepped forward.

Cinema now flows, shifts, and adapts. It grows with every creator bold enough to experiment, every fan who edits a moment they love, every gamer who sees story in motion, and every artist who learns a new tool just to see what happens.

The next wave of film won't rise from one city or one industry. It will rise from bedrooms, classrooms, studios, cafés, gaming chairs, community spaces, and anywhere imagination takes shape.

So before we proceed to the next lot, here are a few sparks to explore: quick, fun, and built to unlock creativity:

Try This:

- Search "first video game ever made" and check how far digital storytelling has come.
- Look up one classic game cinematic and study how emotion carries through animation.
- Experiment with any AI tool you find interesting: image generation, sound cleanup, motion tracking, or video ideas.
- Watch a short film created by an independent creator online.
- Pick a global film you've never heard of and watch the trailer.

A Quick Quiz for Curiosity:

1. What game introduced the first widely recognized open-world structure?
2. Which film used one of the earliest digital doubles in a major scene?
3. What engine powers many modern virtual production stages?

4. Which country produces one of the highest volumes of films annually?

5. Which AI-powered technique helps restore damaged footage?

The future is here, growing wherever someone decides to create something new. Take advantage of it.

THE FINAL FRAME

"Fear is the mind-killer."
— Dune (2021)

"Perfectly balanced… as all stories should be." Thanos spoke those words with a universe in his grasp, yet the line fits this moment more quietly. You've travelled across more than a century of motion, sound, color, rebellion, invention, fandom, digital evolution, and imagination. Now you stand at the edge of it like someone stepping out of a long movie marathon, blinking into the light, realizing how much the world of cinema holds.

What a journey it has been: From trains rushing toward stunned audiences in the silent era to creators launching films on platforms that reach millions overnight, the story of cinema moves with the same energy as the people who shape it. Every new era rose from curiosity. Every breakthrough came from someone who tried something different. Every major shift started as a small idea in someone's hands.

Take a moment to feel the weight of that.

Cameras changed, screens changed, formats changed, but the heart stayed steady: stories grow because people grow. Vision expands when creators expand. Film history is not a museum. It is a living timeline carried forward by everyone who watches, edits, draws, performs, experiments, or builds something from a spark.

The path you walked across these chapters formed more than knowledge. It formed a perspective. You have seen how entire movements began with brave decisions. You have seen how global voices shaped new lanes. You have seen how technology opened doors that once felt locked. The world of cinema widened with each generation, and now it reaches toward you with the same invitation.

The credits aren't rolling because the story is finished; they roll because your scene is about to begin.

And here is the part most people overlook: cinema evolves through bold hands, not perfect ones. Every era you studied carried mistakes, experiments, accidents, risks, and moments that were never guaranteed to work. Yet those moments shaped entire generations of creators. Someone pointed a camera at a place no one cared to film. Someone edited a scene in a way that felt strange at the time. Someone added color when the world thought black and white was enough. Someone uploaded a shaky YouTube video without realizing it would spark a career. Each of those choices advanced the story of cinema.

Imagine what your version of that choice could be.

Maybe you break down a scene and learn why it moves you. Maybe you film something small on your phone and discover a style you never knew you had. Maybe you sketch characters, remix sounds, create edits, react to trailers, study cinematics, or write moments that feel real to you. Every action, no matter how small, becomes part of a much larger thread.

The world no longer waits for permission to create, and neither should you. Your ideas carry the same energy that shaped every movement in film history. Your voice sits in the same continuum as the rebels, the innovators, the animators, the editors, the gamers, the dreamers, and the storytellers who turned their sparks into culture.

You reached the end of this journey, yet you stand at the start of another. The tools exist. The platforms exist. The curiosity exists. The only thing left is the decision to step forward.

Every great film begins with a single moment. This could be yours.

THE CREATOR'S END-GAME — YOUR PERSONAL QUESTLINE

Every great story leaves you with something to carry forward. This is your sandbox, your quest board, your mixtape of sparks. A space to explore, experiment, and unlock whatever feels true to you.

Pick what calls you. Leave what doesn't. Remix everything.

Questline One: Expand Your World

Track 1 — MAPPA Madness

Watch an episode from any MAPPA project. Study how the studio handles motion, emotion, and pacing. Notice how frames hold detail even in explosive scenes.

Purpose: Strengthen your ability to read animation with intention and understand how movement communicates feeling.

Track 2 — A Journey Through Middle-earth

Choose one scene from *The Lord of the Rings* and break down the mood. The music, the lighting, the silence. Ask yourself why it lands every time.

Purpose: Build awareness of cinematic atmosphere and how directors shape emotion without saying a word.

Track 3 — The Force Awakens Again

Rewatch any lightsaber duel from *Star Wars*. Focus on color, rhythm, and choreography. Think about how sound shapes tension.

Purpose: Train your eye to see how action scenes rely on timing, sound, and visual balance.

Track 4 — House of Fire and Frames

Pick your favorite moment from *House of the Dragon*. Pause it. Study where each character stands, how shadows fall, how the room breathes.

Purpose: Learn how blocking, posture, and light shape storytelling in quiet scenes.

Questline Two: Train Your Eye

Mission 1 — Three Shots

Capture three photos or short clips that feel cinematic to you. No context to it, just scenes that carry a mood.

Purpose: Build visual intuition by noticing cinematic potential in everyday spaces.

Mission 2 — One Edit, One Emotion

Use any editing app to craft a tiny clip that conveys a feeling. Joy. Calm. Chaos. Nostalgia. Anything.

Purpose: Strengthen your sense of emotional pacing and rhythm.

Mission 3 — The Frame Hunt

Look for scenes online that match your mood. Collect them like artifacts.

Purpose: Train your eye to recognize visual patterns and stylistic signatures.

Questline Three: Level Up Your Tools

Skill 1 — Explore a Free Platform

Try Blender, CapCut, Procreate, Unreal, or any tool that sparks curiosity. Open one tutorial and follow along.

Purpose: Reduce fear around unfamiliar tools and build technical confidence.

Skill 2 — Experiment with AI

Test any creative AI feature that interests you. Generate a sketch idea, clean dialog, shape lighting, or build concepts.

Purpose: Learn how modern creators use AI as a support system, not a replacement.

Skill 3 — Soundtrack Mode

Add music to a simple clip. See how it transforms the emotion.

Purpose: Understand how sound shifts the tone of a scene.

Questline Four: Join the Culture

Challenge 1 — Anime Energy

Ask a friend for an anime recommendation. Watch one episode. Notice pacing, humor, and heart.

Purpose: Explore how different cultures shape storytelling.

Challenge 2 — Global Lens

Find a film from a country you rarely explore. Watch the trailer. You may discover a new favorite style.

Purpose: Expand your cinematic worldview and recognize global influences.

Challenge 3 — Creator Spotlight

Follow one indie filmmaker or animator online. Study how they build with limited resources.

Purpose: Learn how creativity thrives even without big budgets.

Questline Five: Unlock Your Voice

Path 1 — Write a Scene

Keep it short: A conversation, a moment, or a decision.

Purpose: Strengthen your storytelling instincts through simplicity.

Path 2 — Build a World

Sketch or describe a location where your story takes place.

Purpose: Train your imagination to think in setting, tone, and detail.

Path 3 — Craft a Character

Give them a goal, a flaw, and something they care about.

Purpose: Develop your sense of emotional structure and character depth.

Questline Six: Final Boss Mode

Pick one fandom and dive deeper.

- *Attack on Titan* for intensity.
- *Star Wars* for myth and legacy.
- *The Lord of the Rings* for heart and heroism.

- *House of the Dragon* for power and politics.
- Any MAPPA project for animation excellence.

Study how the creators built tension, emotion, and identity into their worlds.

Purpose: Understand how world-building and theme shape entire universes and how fan culture keeps them alive.

Ultimately, every legendary saga ends with a choice that carries the hero forward, and this is yours.

Pick one idea from this page and chase it in whatever form feels natural to you, whether it becomes a frame you capture, a sound you reshape, a feeling you follow, a sketch you explore, a clip you refine, or a thought you choose to grow. Creation often begins as one small spark that you decide to keep alive.

So as the screen fades, the world widens. Some worlds are watched, some worlds are built, but you carry the tools to build your own now.

Fade out… then rise.

THE REEL STARTER PACK

This is your personal vault, your mixtape of worlds to explore, the starting lineup of films that shaped eras, defined genres, and inspired creators across the globe. No pressure to watch them all at once. No order required. Drop into whatever calls your name and let curiosity lead. Each section carries ten films that represent a feeling, a movement, a breakthrough, or a spark. Treat this as a map, not a checklist.

1. The Originals — Foundations of Film

Stories that built the language of cinema. Pure visual instinct and invention.

1. *The Kid* (1921) – Charlie Chaplin's heart and humor.
2. *Nosferatu* (1922) – A masterclass in atmosphere.
3. *Metropolis* (1927) – Sci-fi before sci-fi existed.
4. *The Jazz Singer* (1927) – Sound enters the chat.
5. *City Lights* (1931) – Emotion through movement.
6. *Frankenstein* (1931) – The birth of monster cinema.
7. *Modern Times* (1936) – Industry meets comedy.

8. *Snow White and the Seven Dwarfs* (1937) – Animation finds its voice.
9. *The Wizard of Oz* (1939) – Color becomes fantasy.
10. *Gone With the Wind* (1939) – A giant of early Hollywood.

2. The Game Changers — Films That Shifted the Culture

Rebels, rule-breakers, and experiments that changed everything.

1. *Citizen Kane* (1941) – The blueprint for modern filmmaking.
2. *Bicycle Thieves* (1948) – Real life on screen.
3. *Rashomon* (1950) – One story, many truths.
4. *Seven Samurai* (1954) – Action storytelling perfected.
5. *Psycho* (1960) – Suspense redefined.
6. *2001: A Space Odyssey* (1968) – Cinema becomes cosmic.
7. *Taxi Driver* (1976) – Urban storytelling with heat.
8. *Rocky* (1976) – Underdog energy.
9. *Star Wars* (1977) – Myth, magic, and world-building.
10. *Apocalypse Now* (1979) – Scale, ambition, intensity.

3. The Icons — Movies Every Fan Should Experience Once

Blockbusters, fantasy worlds, animated magic, epic emotions.

1. *The Empire Strikes Back* (1980)
2. *The Shining* (1980)
3. *E.T. the Extra-Terrestrial* (1982)
4. *Akira* (1988)
5. *The Lion King* (1994)

6. *The Shawshank Redemption* (1994)
7. *Princess Mononoke* (1997)
8. *The Matrix* (1999)
9. *Spirited Away* (2001)
10. *The Lord of the Rings: The Fellowship of the Ring* (2001)

4. Global Gems — Stories From Every Corner of the World

Cinema without borders. Styles shaped by culture and community.

1. *Tsotsi* (2005) – South Africa
2. *District 9* (2009) – South Africa
3. *City of God* (2002) – Brazil
4. *Pan's Labyrinth* (2006) – Mexico/Spain
5. *Crouching Tiger, Hidden Dragon* (2000) – China/Taiwan
6. *Parasite* (2019) – South Korea
7. *Train to Busan* (2016) – South Korea
8. *Amélie* (2001) – France
9. *Roma* (2018) – Mexico
10. *Spirited Away* (2001) – Japan (global masterpiece)

5. The New Age — Modern Must-Watch Stories

Streaming-era heat, bold experiments, new voices, global vision.

1. *Black Panther* (2018)
2. *Everything Everywhere All at Once* (2022)
3. *Dune* (2021)
4. *Spider-Man: Into the Spider-Verse* (2018)
5. *The Social Network* (2010)
6. *Get Out* (2017)

7. *Her* (2013)

8. *The Last of Us* (2023) – storytelling across mediums

9. *RRR* (2022)

10. *Top Gun: Maverick* (2022)

You don't need to start at the beginning or finish the list or even agree with every choice. This playlist is just a recommendation for exploration. Choose based on mood, curiosity, energy, or instinct.

Every film here shaped, inspired, or challenged someone. You may find one that sparks something in you. Press play on whatever calls you. The reel moves forward from here.

REFERENCES

Agnès Varda† – EGS – Division of Philosophy, Art, and Critical Thought. (2019). Egs.edu. https://pact.egs.edu/biography/agnes-varda%E2%80%A0/

An alternative introduction to 21st-Century Japanese cinema. (2023, November 13). Arrow Films. https://www.arrowfilms.com/blog/uncategorized/an-alternative-introduction-to-21st-century-japanese-cinema/

Barney, N., Yasar, K., & Wigmore, I. (2025, May 22). *What is deepfake technology?* WhatIs. com. https://www.techtarget.com/whatis/definition/deepfake

Barson, M. (2025, October 14). *Ida Lupino | Biography, movies, & facts.* Encyclopedia Britannica. https://www.britannica.com/biography/Ida-Lupino

Braun , S. (2025). *Streaming in 2025 vs. 2035: The evolution of Seamless TV.* 24i.com. https://www.24i.com/blogs/the-consumers-wishlist-what-a-seamless-streaming-experience-looks-like-in-2035

Cook, D. A., & Sklar, R. (2025 18). *History of film | Summary, industry, history, technology, directors, & facts.* Encyclopedia Britannica. https://www.britannica.com/art/history-of-film/International-cinema

Davis, J. (2016, October 21). *Say it loud! The black cinema revolution.* Harvard Film Archive. https://harvardfilmarchive.org/programs/say-it-loud-the-black-cinema-revolution

Davis, J. (2021, April 15). *Blaxploitation and the evolution of Black Films.* The Tiger's Roar. https://www.tigersroar.com/article_da5f3cc8-9e03-11eb-a2d4-232073e9c534.html

Harries, S. (n.d.). *What Is the Japanese New Wave?* Movements in Film. https://www.movementsinfilm.com/japanese-new-wave

Heckmann, C. (2019, November 11). *What Is Italian Neorealism in Film? Defining the Style*. StudioBinder. https://www.studiobinder.com/blog/what-is-italian-neorealism-in-film/

History.com Editors. (2009, November 13). *Pioneering Nickelodeon theater opens*. HISTORY. https://www.history.com/this-day-in-history/June-19/first-nickelodeon-opens

Hollywood's transition to sound. (n.d.). Cinecollage. http://cinecollage.net/hollywood-transition.html

Italian Neorealism. (n.d.). Movements in Film. https://www.movementsinfilm.com/italian-neorealism

Jivkova, K. (2021, November 14). *Benshi performance in the Japanese silent film era*. Retrospect Journal. https://retrospectjournal.com/2021/11/14/benshi-performance-in-the-japanese-silent-film-era/

Kane, A. J. (2025, April 29). *Understanding LED Volume Technology for Immersive Productions*. Avixa Portal. https://www.avixa.org/pro-av-trends/articles/led-volume-for-immersive-productions

Maio, A. (2015, August 1). *Watch: Directing techniques of the French New Wave*. StudioBinder. https://www.studiobinder.com/blog/what-is-french-new-wave/

Pfeiffer, L. (n.d.). The Jazz Singer | film by Crosland [1927]. In *Encyclopædia Britannica*. https://www.britannica.com/topic/The-Jazz-Singer-film-1927

Satchell-Baeza, S. (2019, October 21). *A profile of Shirley Clarke*. BFI. https://www.bfi.org.uk/sight-and-sound/features/shirley-clarke-career-profile-filmography

Shao, J. (2024). The evolution of film technology in the streaming media era. *Lecture Notes in Education Psychology and Public Media, 37*(1), 89–93. https://doi.org/10.54254/2753-7048/37/20240509

Sharp, J. (2017, January 27). *Where to begin with the Japanese New Wave*. BFI. https://www.bfi.org.uk/features/where-begin-japanese-new-wave

Shirley Clarke. (2015). The Museum of Modern Art; MoMA. https://www.moma.org/artists/32202-shirley-clarke

Sims, Y. (2019). Blaxploitation movies. In *Encyclopædia Britannica*. https://www.britannica.com/art/blaxploitation-movie

Smith, K. (2012, October 12). *A Trip to the Penny Arcade - Circa 1907*. Blogspot. http://allincolorforaquarter.blogspot.com/2012/10/a-trip-to-penny-arcade-circa-1907.html

The Magic Lantern Society. (n.d.). Magiclantern. https://www.magiclantern.org.uk/

Tikkanen, A. (n.d.). *Why are hit movies called blockbusters? | Military, World War II, Hollywood, bombs, & facts*. Encyclopedia Britannica. https://www.britannica.com/topic/Why-Are-Hit-Movies-Called-Blockbusters

Victorian optical toys. (2018, January 12). Happening History. https://happeninghistory.co.uk/victorian-optical-toys/

What is Genre? (n.d.). BBC Bitesize. https://www.bbc.co.uk/bitesize/articles/zv73vwx#z32b3j6

Where to begin with Agnès Varda. (2018, May 23). BFI. https://www.bfi.org.uk/features/where-begin-with-agnes-varda